THE HAMPSTEAD SYNAGOGUE 1892-1967

THE HAMPSTEAD SYNAGOGUE

1892-1967

"For some things concession,
in most things conciliation,
above all things union."

—*Herbert Bentwich*

by
RAYMOND APPLE

Published to mark the 75th anniversary of the establishment
of the congregation.

VALLENTINE, MITCHELL · LONDON

First published in Great Britain by
Vallentine, Mitchell & Co. Ltd.
18 Cursitor Street, London, E.C.4

© *1967 The Hampstead Synagogue*
© *1967 illustrations: The Hampstead Synagogue*

Printed and Bound in Great Britain
by Tonbridge Printers Ltd., Tonbridge, Kent.

CONTENTS

ILLUSTRATIONS

This history is dedicated
by his wife and sons
to the memory of

SIMON DU PARC BRAHAM
(1889–1966)

who worshipped at the Hampstead Synagogue
all his life

Generous contributions
towards the publication of this book
have also been made
in memory of

HARRY RONALD JACOBS
LEOPOLD LAZARUS
REBECCA SILVERSTONE
ELEANOR MAY SOLOMON

Introduction

SYNAGOGUE HISTORIES ARE rarely significant contributions to historical knowledge or of any importance to people outside the immediate membership of the congregation and those who remember the worshippers of an earlier generation. That fact in itself ought to have made the present writer think twice or three times before embarking upon a project of this kind.

The temptation so often is to record the small details of a congregation's history, its procession of ministers and lay leaders and the milestones in its building, without making the attempt or, indeed, even possessing the ability to relate them to the broad sweep of events and movements in the corresponding periods in Jewish and general history. The reader may well decide that, judged against this ambitious standard, this record of the Hampstead Synagogue is not an adequate work of history. But it must be said that there is a uniqueness about the foundation and character of Hampstead which does provide the historian with a great opportunity.

Hampstead has always been more than simply a local house of worship established for Jewish residents in a particular district of London, even though the Jewish population of West Hampstead was growing so rapidly at the end of the nineteenth century that sooner or later a Synagogue would inevitably have been built to cater for them. The men who founded Hampstead were men of unusual personality and ideals, and living in an age of religious restlessness they set out not only to erect a building but to initiate a religious movement.

1

In that sense the three years preceding the actual opening of the Synagogue in 1892 were of more than ordinary significance, and through the publicity and controversy which attended them one is able to gauge to what extent the ideals of 'the Hampstead movement' reached fulfilment in the context of the Anglo-Jewish religious establishment as it then was.

Some of the pragmatic points in the programme of the founders of the Synagogue did not receive the rabbinical sanction that was necessary before they could be put into practice, yet it is not a simple matter of saying, as one view had it, that 'the promoters of the Hampstead Synagogue were, almost to a man, unanimously agreed upon reform, and formally appealed for it. Their demands were refused. They instantly succumbed. The few independent minds among them carried out those reforms (elsewhere).' This claim was made in 1892 by Oswald John Simon,[1] an amateur theologian of the time who supported the 'independent minds' who broke away from the Hampstead movement when its full programme was not sanctioned by the Chief Rabbi.

His dissatisfaction was not shared by all the members of the movement. In a reply to Oswald John Simon, Herbert Bentwich, who had brought the movement into being, declared: 'The leaders of the true Hampstead movement, and with them the bulk of the Committee, have adhered, as I hope they will continue to adhere, to the principle that in matters of ritual there is no reform which can outweigh in importance that abiding principle of Judaism – the maintenance of Union.'[2] Bentwich was a complex character, and his views should not be over-simplified, but the attitude he probably shared with a sizeable number of his colleagues was that, despite the limitations imposed by circumstances, there were still ideals which Hampstead could pioneer and demonstrate to others.

Even Bentwich eventually left the Synagogue in disillusionment, feeling as others have done, both then and in later years, that far from becoming a dynamic movement, Hampstead had developed into a citadel of prosperous respectability. But we with the benefit of hindsight can still discern that some distinctive features have been characteristic of Hampstead from the beginning.

Apart from the very high standard of organisation and conduct of services, which has brought the Synagogue its justified reputation for dignity, decorum and devotion, the initiative for charitable, social, cultural and religious movements has frequently arisen from Hampstead. The leaders of the congregation, clergy and laity, have often been men of independent ideas, and among the large membership there have always been many distinguished figures in Jewish and public life. A leaven of non-conformity has always characterised Hampstead, yet on the whole extremes have not been favoured and at times the most non-conformist feature of Hampstead has been its 'middle-of-the-road' approach. In that sense, therefore, something of the progressive idealism of 1889 has been realised.

The fact that the liturgical modifications requested in the early years were not all granted has an importance of its own. It is significant that it was on pragmatic matters like Synagogue ritual and liturgy that many of the controversies in nineteenth-century Anglo-Jewry were based. Inevitably there had to come a time when something much more radical, in the true sense of going more deeply to the root of things, would be seen to follow logically from these more minor agitations, and when the advocates of religious modification could no longer be accommodated within the established form of Judaism. This result came about with the Jewish Religious Union, founded in 1902, and compared to its radical attitude on such questions as the authority of the Bible and the need to observe the Commandments, the Hampstead movement may fittingly be described as non-revolutionary.

If one important criterion by which to study Hampstead is the extent to which it was a movement and not just a house of worship, a second criterion is the effect of geographical factors on the development of the congregation. The original publicity material prepared for potential members of the Synagogue declared: 'The site is excellently situated in the main road, is central for the West Hampstead, Finchley, Frognal, North Kilburn, Brondesbury, Cricklewood and Willesden districts, and is in a neighbourhood in which the number of Jewish residents is constantly and rapidly increasing.' Most of the original members lived in Kilburn, St. John's Wood and West Hampstead, in the area bounded by the west side of the Finchley Road, though some came from further afield in other districts of north-west London.

The opening of the Brondesbury Synagogue in 1905 and later of Synagogues in other parts of north-west London had little immediate effect on Hampstead, which now, instead of having an *over*-large membership, merely had a *very* large one. Until shortly after the first World War Jewish families lived in large numbers in the immediate vicinity of the Synagogue, particularly in the streets off West End Lane, but now it became difficult to maintain the large houses and members began removing from the district. Their houses became, and in many cases have remained, divided into flats. At this period the N.W.3 area of Hampstead proper on the other side of the Finchley Road was not yet as heavily populated with Jewish families as it has become since the second World War, and in the late 1920's and early 1930's what rescued the Synagogue from possible decline was the opening of the Hocroft Estate, N.W.2, between West Hampstead and Cricklewood, with its more manageable family houses.

In recent years a large proportion of Synagogue members have come from Hampstead proper, for whom the Hampstead and the Hampstead Garden Suburb Synagogues are roughly equidistant. Some families with a long association with Hampstead have retained their membership after moving completely out of the district; hence a significant minority of members live outside north-west London, some as far away as Switzerland, Sweden and the U.S.A. On the whole there has been no significant change in the economic or social character of the membership : now, as in the 1890's, it is mostly a middle-class membership, with a large minority of professional people.

A further aspect which deserves attention is the atmosphere during services in the Synagogue. A recent guide to London, in a chapter on 'Jewish London', praises the quality of the sermons and the cantorial and choral music at Hampstead as the best in any of the London Synagogues, but suggests that Hampstead's decorum goes with a cold, unfriendly attitude.[3] This kind of judgment is necessarily subjective, but those who are able to compare Hampstead today with what it was two generations ago agree that there is a greater warmth about the congregation today, and that the old snobbishness of which Hampstead was accused is almost entirely a thing of the past.

The dignity and decorum, so long the proud boasts of the congregation, are maintained, but sartorially there has been a great change in the last thirty years. No longer are silk hats and frock coats *de rigueur* on Sabbaths, and dinner jackets or full evening dress on Kol Nidre night; nor are Bar Mitzvah boys attired in silk hats and Eton suits.

The somewhat patronising attitude which once marked Hampstead's work for Jewish immigrants has completely gone : many members are themselves former refugees from Central Europe or the descendants of immigrants from Eastern Europe. The regular weekly *kiddush* and the gatherings on such occasions as Sukkoth and Simchath Torah help to promote a spirit of friendliness, and the opening of the community centre was a most important landmark in this respect. Hampstead is not what is colloquially called

5

'heimish', but its members would strongly resent being called cold and unfriendly.

The seventy-fifth anniversary of the opening of the Synagogue calls for celebration for many reasons. In the first place, both the twenty-fifth and the fiftieth anniversaries occurred during wartime, and on both occasions any large-scale celebration would have been out of the question (though each time a special service was held and a pamphlet history published, written by the late Dr. Jacob Snowman, to whose work the present writer is happy to pay tribute). But even more important than that, the attainment of the age of seventy-five is a milestone which, if a human being's life provides any comparison, is normally associated with mellowness and a gradual decline in one's powers. There are even some institutions which, if they reach seventy-five years of history, must be admitted to be monuments to another age rather than being active, lively and forward-looking.

The main question-mark on this seventy-fifth anniversary of Hampstead is the challenge of honest appraisal. Are we to say *ichabod* – the glory is gone? Or is there still enough activity and vitality to weather another 75 years or even longer? The answer to that question may well depend on one's reading of this history, and if it spurs on the present members of the congregation to ensure a dynamic continuity for their Synagogue, the author will be well content.

It only remains to acknowledge the helpful advice and assistance received from the officers of the congregation and from a number of its leading members, present and past. To mention by name those who deserve thanks would perhaps be invidious. I can only venture the humble hope that they find this small work worthy of the Synagogue they love.

May 1967   Raymond Apple

Foundation stone laying for board room and classrooms, 1897. (Central group left to right): L. J. Greenberg, the Rev. S. Manne, Frank I. Lyons, Samuel Moses, Herbert Bentwich, the Rev. A. A. Green, Alexander Jacob

Early interior of the Synagogue

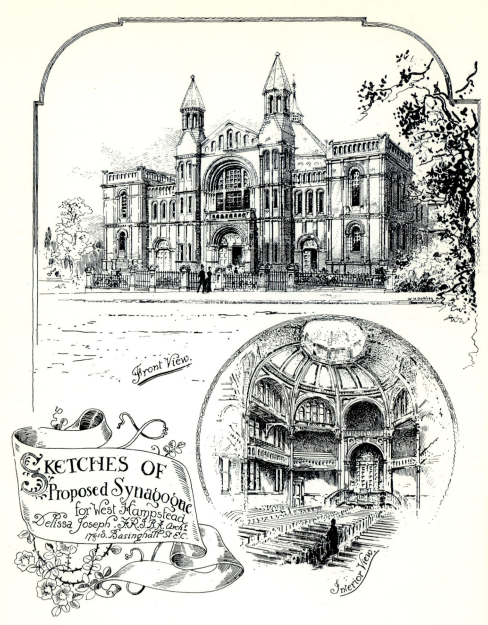

Front View.

Sketches of Proposed Synagogue for West Hampstead. Delissa Joseph. F.R.I.B.A. Arch.t 17&18 Basinghall St E.C.

Interior View.

The original architect's sketches

CHAPTER I

In The Beginning

THE DISTRICT OF Hampstead is of long lineage. A document dating from the year 978 purports to be a grant of the manor of Hamestede by the Crown under Edgar the Peaceable to his minister Mangoda.[1] But there have been periods in subsequent centuries when the character of Hampstead was anything but distinguished. At one time it was notorious for highwaymen, and felons were hanged on Hampstead Heath. At the time of Henry VIII it was a small village chiefly known for its washer-women, to whom the clothes of upper-class Londoners were brought to be washed.

By the late seventeenth century, however, its air and waters had been found to be beneficial to health, and after a physician, Dr. Gibbons, praised the water from springs on the site of the Well Walk of today, the crowds came flocking and water from Hampstead was sold in flasks at the best public establishments and coffee houses. Now Hampstead became a fashionable watering place. A writer in 1735 called it 'one of the Politest Public Places in England' and Daniel Defoe waxed lyrical about it. The new character of the district is well summed up in this extract from William Howitt's 'The Northern Heights of London', published a century ago :

This 'has always been a favourite resort of Londoners, and a favourite abode of commercial and professional men. Lawyers and artists have shown a great preference for it. In times past a considerable number of the nobility had houses there . . . and literary men sought there retirement from the distractions of London. The great number of old brick houses standing in their ample grounds, and gardens enclosed by high brick walls, and shaded by large and lofty elms, show how favourite a place it has been to wealthy merchants, bankers, and others engaged in the commerce and professions of the metropolis.'[2]

Jews must have been amongst the families who settled in Hampstead, for Defoe wrote in 1724 that the 'Jews have particularly fixt upon this town for their country retreat, and some of them are very wealthy; they live there in good figure, and have several Trades particularly depending upon them, and especially Butchers of their own to supply them with provisions kill'd in their own way : also, I am told, they have a private Synagogue here.'[3] It may well be that this private Synagogue belonged to the wealthy Mendes da Costa family, who were descended from Portuguese Marranos and who had houses both in the City and in the Highgate-Hampstead area. Apart from them, however, very little is known of Jewish residents in Hampstead at this period, and Defoe's account is certainly exaggerated.[4]

In 1781 a certain Mrs. Foa (an Italian-Jewish name) was buried in Hampstead parish churchyard at the age of 110, and at the same time a controversialist called Abraham Abrahams lived in Hampstead, but official records of Hampstead contain hardly any unmistakably Jewish names.[5] The first Jew of whom we have much information as having lived in the district is Eliezer Isaac Keyser, who was born in Amsterdam in 1746, became a prominent member of the Great Synagogue and was a prosperous merchant in the City of London. In 1812, after he had twice been left a widower, he retired to Hampstead. He got on well with his neighbours, but felt his isolation from Jewish life deeply, and as long as he was able he always made the effort to go to town to observe the festivals.

When his son Isaac died in 1817, Keyser sat *shivah* in the City. By the following winter he was unwell himself. He observed Yom Kippur at home, and relatives sent him *arba'ah minim* for the festival of Sukkoth. In 1820 he prepared to celebrate a lonely Passover in Hampstead. But before that Passover arrived he died, aged 74, and was interred in London in the burial ground of the Great Synagogue.[6]

Seventy years later, however, Hampstead was no more a lonely place for a Jew to live. The Jewish community was no longer almost entirely centred on the City. Jews had moved to the West End and Bayswater, and after a protracted struggle with the authorities of the historic City Synagogues, they had obtained permission to establish places of worship in these new areas of Jewish residence. Hence the Central Synagogue, Great Portland Street, was founded in 1855 as a branch of the Great, and the Bayswater Synagogue, Chichester Place, in 1863 as a branch of the Great and the New Synagogues jointly.

With the establishment of the United Synagogue in 1870 it became possible to erect Synagogues where they were needed, and not only did the historic congregations no longer oppose such schemes but, because of the principle of mutuality on which the United Synagogue was based, assistance could be given to ensure that new congregations were established on a sound footing.

The St. John's Wood Synagogue was the first to cater for the move northwards by Jewish families,[7] and by the end of the 1880's Jews were living in some numbers in St. John's Wood and beyond, in Kilburn and West Hampstead, though not as yet in Hampstead proper. They included some notable figures in the fields of art and culture – Israel Abrahams, Herbert Bentwich, Arthur Davis, Joseph Jacobs, Morris Joseph, Asher I. Myers, Solomon Schechter, Solomon J. Solomon, Lucien Wolf and Israel Zangwill. Many of them were connected with 'The Wanderers', a circle of intellectuals dominated by the personality and learning of Solomon Schechter. Norman Bentwich wrote of them : 'The Wanderers were a kind of Fourth Party in Anglo-Jewry, concerned to make Judaism a living force, and in arms against the com-

B

placent respectability of both the lay and spiritual leaders.'[8]

It was a period of religious restlessness. Some thought that the salvation of Judaism could be ensured by modifying the ritual and liturgy of the Synagogue. Attempts in this direction had been matters of communal controversy on several occasions in the previous two decades. The Rev. Aaron Levy Green of the Central Synagogue had long been advocating revision both in his sermons and also in his regular contributions, signed with the pen-name 'Nemo', in the 'Jewish Chronicle'. A brilliant young undergraduate, Numa Hartog, had publicly challenged Nathan Marcus Adler, the Chief Rabbi, to justify the observance of the second days of the festivals. Walter Josephs had set up an Association for Effecting a Modification in the Liturgy of the German Jews. The 'Jewish World' published articles in support of the movement, and these were reprinted and distributed throughout the Empire.

In 1879 a conference of Synagogues put proposals for change before Adler, to some of which he acceded, though with the utmost reluctance. But the advocates of change were not completely satisfied. Throughout the following decade they pressed their claims. Now, with the increasing Jewish migration to West Hampstead, the association of many local residents with the progressive movement, and the powerful proportions which the agitation was reaching, the determination arose to launch a scheme for a place of worship in Hampstead which would not be quite of the United Synagogue type but would be an institution *sui generis*.

The first move came from Herbert Bentwich, a lawyer who lived in Abbey Road, St. John's Wood, and was a member of the St. John's Wood Synagogue and a passionate participant in every congregational controversy. When St. John's Wood was considering minor changes in Synagogue procedure, Bentwich threw himself into a movement of protest against the 'increasing Anglican propriety' of the Synagogue. (He may well have shared Solomon Schechter's

10

disdain for the 'red-tape or flunkey Judaism' of the staid establishment). He was dissatisfied with St. John's Wood on a number of counts and it seems that he hoped that a new Synagogue in Hampstead could bring about a revival based on 'Jewish influences' and eliminating 'external' influences. His views were not identical with those who wanted out-and-out ritual reform, and it was inevitable that eventually things should come to a head and the two groups part company.

Bentwich wrote a letter to the 'Jewish Chronicle' in May, 1889, inviting support for the idea of a Synagogue in Hampstead. On 30th May he convened a meeting at the West Hampstead Town Hall, Broadhurst Gardens, at which it was decided 'that the gentlemen present constitute themselves into a provisional committee (with power to add to their number) for the purpose of ascertaining the desirability of establishing forthwith a Synagogue in the Hampstead district.'

Those present were: Israel Abrahams, Herbert Bentwich, Edward P. Davis, Maurice Davis, Louis Davis, Michael A. Green, Percy L. Isaac, A. A. Jones, Ernest D. Löwy, Frank I. Lyons, Louis Schlesinger, David Solomon, and M. Woolf. Eight others were unable to be present, but expressed willingness to serve on the provisional committee. They were: Lionel Davis, A. Lindo Henry, Alfred Henry, Henry H. Hyams, Samuel Moses, Bernard Solomon, George Vandamm and L. Weiss, and other names were added to the list at almost every meeting.

The original committee included members of all the three congregational bodies then in existence – the United Synagogue, the Spanish and Portuguese Synagogue and the Berkeley Street Reform Synagogue. Their ambition was to launch a movement which would be somewhere between Orthodoxy and Reform, and for two months they met very frequently to work out a scheme of services for the proposed Synagogue. The main innovations to emerge were:

11

1. Two services would be held on Sabbath mornings, the early morning service at 8.30 a.m. and the second service (commencing from the *Nishmath* prayer) at 11 a.m. (In some other Synagogues the services were also divided but with only a brief interval between them.)
2. All repetitions of prayers, including the Sabbath *Amidoth*, would be omitted.
3. The *duchan* ceremony or 'blessings of the Priests' would be abolished, as was the custom of some provincial congregations.
4. The Ten Commandments would be read every Sabbath.
5. A small part of the service would be read in English.
6. A service for the confirmation of girls would be held.

In addition it was decided to adopt a number of other improvements in the conduct of services which had been customary for some years even in Synagogues under the Chief Rabbi's jurisdiction, for example the omission of a special *mi sheberach* for each individual called to the Torah.

In the discussions which led up to the final report of the Committee some widely divergent opinions were expressed, and it is clear that a sizeable minority of members would have preferred something more radical. Some wanted a triennial cycle of reading the Torah.[9] When this was rejected, it was suggested that instead of the whole of the weekly *sidra* being read, a selection should be made from it, but this too was narrowly defeated.

There were various views as to the reading of part of the service in English, and it was finally decided that one or two Psalms, a portion of the Prophets and the Prayer for the Royal Family should be read in English. The Committee was equally divided as to whether it was desirable to have an organ as an adjunct to the service, but the decision (by a majority of four to three) taken in the end was that it would be 'inexpedient' to recommend this at the present time.

Herbert Bentwich was in the chair at the meetings at which

these points were debated, and it was often necessary for him to exercise a casting vote. On the whole it was the status quo which his vote maintained. Writing in the 'Jewish Chronicle' some time later, he expressed his belief that 'in matters of ritual there is no reform which can outweigh in importance that abiding principle of Judaism – the maintenance of Union.'[10] In some handwritten notes of his which have been preserved, his view is again clearly expressed: 'To those who started the movement it was not for the purpose of having something sensational in ritual or magnificent in building – but they desired to supply religious requirements the urgency of which was even then acknowledged.'

At an early stage Frank I. Lyons proposed that the congregation should accept the authority of the Chief Rabbi, though with a revised service. But the question was left in abeyance until the scheme of services was completed. Now, on 17th July, a meeting decided unanimously: 'That before the Committee proceed to canvass for support in the district it is expedient to decide under which ecclesiastical authorities, if any, the proposed Synagogue shall be placed.' Five voted in favour of an association with the Reform Synagogue, but nine opposed it.

Michael A. Green then moved and John Meredith seconded a resolution: 'That subject to the modifications involved in the general principles adopted by the Committee as regards the Service, the ritual of the proposed Synagogue be that known as the German Minhag and that steps be forthwith taken to place the proposed Synagogue under the supervision of the Chief Rabbi.' This was carried with one dissentient, presumably F. H. Harvey-Samuel, who tendered his resignation soon afterwards 'as he did not feel justified in assisting to establish a Synagogue which he considered orthodox.'

Like that of Harvey-Samuel, the 'Jewish Chronicle's' view was that: 'The programme partakes of the character of a declaration of orthodoxy and a protest against Reform. The

13

Committee are at the pains of affirming that the Synagogue is to be open on the second days of the festivals, that they do not intend to have an organ, and that they do intend to retain the existing system of reading the Law ... The innovations which the Committee would introduce are neither numerous nor revolutionary.'[11]

A deputation of members of the executive went on 25th July to put the proposals before Hermann Adler, the Delegate Chief Rabbi, who promised to convey them to his father, the Chief Rabbi, but said that a reply could not be expected before the end of October. The Committee had intended to hold High Holyday services at the West Hampstead Town Hall 'strictly upon the lines of the programme adopted by the General Committee,' with the Rev. Morris Joseph officiating, but out of respect to the Chief Rabbi it was now agreed not to go ahead with this plan for the time being.

The promised reply came in a letter dated 24th October from Nathan Marcus Adler to Ernest D. Löwy, honorary secretary of the Hampstead Committee. The reply was also published in full in the 'Jewish Chronicle' of 1st November. It was seen that the Chief Rabbi was not prepared to sanction some of the most basic points of the committee's programme. He consented to a second service at 11 o'clock, but it was not to commence with *Nishmath* but with *Ein Kamocha*. Some minor repetitions of prayers could be omitted, but the Sabbath *Amidoth* had to be repeated. *Duchaning* was not to be abolished. The reading of the Ten Commandments was not to be a part of the regular Sabbath service. No English prayers were permitted except the prayer for the Royal Family and certain supplementary Bible readings. A special service for girls might be held, but it must not be called 'confirmation'.

At a meeting on 10th November bitter criticism was directed at the Chief Rabbi's refusal to depart from the laws of the *Shulchan Aruch*. Frank I. Lyons moved that further

14

discussion on the details of the ritual be deferred until the proposed Synagogue had been built and that plans for the erection of the Synagogue be proceeded with 'on the basis that the congregation shall be under the ministerial guidance of the Chief Rabbi, with a revised service.' A majority of members were prepared to accept this compromise, but Michael A. Green (son of the Rev. A. L. Green and cousin of the Rev. A. A. Green) and Percy L. Isaac now moved :

'That the programme of the proposed Hampstead Synagogue having failed to obtain the sanction of the Revd. the Chief Rabbi, this committee is now freed from its pledge to support such programme if sanctioned by him and in order to ensure perfect liberty of action for all members individually or collectively this committee do now dissolve.'

Eight voted for and eight against. A critical position had arisen. The chairman, Herbert Bentwich, had the casting vote. He voted against the resolution, with the effect that the committee remained in existence. But now the eight dissentients walked out. The same day they addressed a letter to Bentwich resigning from the committee and stating :

'We withdrew from the meeting, considering that any action other than dissolution would have been contrary to the letter and the spirit of the resolutions under which the movement was founded, and subsequently carried on, and would have been at variance with the understanding arrived at with a view of reconciling divergent opinions.'

These eight – Israel Abrahams, M. J. Alexander, Edward P. Davis, Michael A. Green, Bernhard F. Halford, A. Lindo Henry, Percy L. Isaac and George Vandamm – were joined the following day by the honorary secretary, Ernest D. Löwy, who was a member of the Reform Synagogue. In his letter of resignation Löwy told Bentwich : 'I do not feel justified in

15

assisting a movement with which I am not in entire sympathy'. In his place Samuel Moses became honorary secretary.

The executive now made a further approach to Hermann Adler in the hope of saving some at least of the original proposals. Reporting to the committee on 30th November, Frank I. Lyons was able to state that a 'satisfactory result' had emerged from the discussions with Hermann Adler, who apparently felt that some further concessions could be made in order to save the situation. Lyons said that permission was given to start the second service with *Nishmath* or *Barechu* instead of with *Ein Kamocha,* provided this service began at about 10 o'clock instead of at 11. Secondly, 'as to the *Amidah,* its repetition in the service was not vital to Judaism', and further, 'it was in the power of the Committee of the Synagogue, after its establishment, to make alterations in the method of the recital of the blessings of the *Kohanim,* subject to an appeal by any member of the congregation to the Chief Rabbi.'

While none of these concessions explicitly contradicted the Chief Rabbi's reply of 24th October, they were sufficiently lenient to provide a possible basis for the restoration of peace and for the original principles of the movement to be maintained, while still acting 'under the ministerial guidance of the Chief Rabbi.' While it is not easy to discover what official status, if any, these discussions with Hermann Adler had, and whether he was binding the Chief Rabbinate or simply stating his own personal views, Hermann Adler did (as we shall see) honour these points in 1892 when, as his father's successor, he presided over a conference on the subject of modifications in the ritual.

The meeting on 30th November, after hearing Lyons' report, felt that it might now be possible to persuade the members who had resigned to return, but Lyons said that he had already tried this without success, and before long eleven new members joined the committee in place of the secessionists.

16

A number of the latter were already busily engaged in organising a more radical movement in the district. The 'Jewish Chronicle' of 20th December announced plans for a Sabbath afternoon service in Hampstead 'so framed as to meet the wants of those who are not *en rapport* with the present form of public worship.' There would be a modified *Minchah* service in Hebrew, with a Scriptural reading, a psalm and prayer in English and a sermon.[12] A mixed choir of male and female voices would lead the congregational singing, accompanied by an organ. The Rev. Morris Joseph would officiate regularly, and occasional addresses would be given by Israel Abrahams, Claude Goldsmid Montefiore and Oswald John Simon.[13]

The provisional committee comprised M. J. Alexander, Edward P. Davis, Michael A. Green, Bernhard F. Halford, Frederick B. Halford, F. H. Harvey-Samuel, Percy L. Isaac, Maurice Myers and Henry Van den Bergh, with A. Lindo Henry as honorary secretary. Most of them were former members of the Hampstead movement. They made it clear that, in arranging the Sabbath afternoon services, they were interested in starting a trend, not in establishing a Synagogue, and they did not wish to compete with or harm in any way the plans of the committee of the Hampstead Synagogue.

Their services commenced in 1890 and were held first at the West Hampstead Town Hall and later, when permission to use United Synagogue premises was refused, at the Kilburn Town Hall.[14] They continued until 1893. The precise relationship between these services and the Hampstead Synagogue was complex: some supporters of the one also took a leading part in the other, and there were some who felt it might still be possible to bring about an official reconciliation of the two. This was shown particularly in the wish of many people that when the Synagogue was established the Rev. Morris Joseph should become its minister.

As events were to show, it was an over-optimistic thought. Morris Joseph claimed in his book, 'The Ideal in Judaism',

17

which was a collection of sermons preached at the Sabbath afternoon services, that the 'range of doctrine taught at the Hampstead services ... was rarely polemical'. But in some outspoken addresses he expressed views which were hardly calculated to win the approval of the religious establishment, and this was particularly the case with a controversial sermon on 'The Sacrificial Rite' which he describes as 'a rite, from the mere thought of which the best minds recoil with a shudder today ... We could not even tolerate sacrifices; we shrink from them in repulsion.' He added: 'The sooner such outworn, misused elements are eliminated from religion, the better it will be for religion; and those who sweep them away, instead of being stoned as heretics, ought to be crowned as faithful and far-sighted leaders.'[15] Morris Joseph's independence of thought and utterance was to have its repercussions before long.

In the meantime, the Hampstead committee had been having unofficial discussions with the independent Western Synagogue, then in St. Alban's Place, Haymarket, with a view to the Western transferring, with its officials and assets, to Hampstead. The negotiations with the Western went on for some months but finally came to nothing, probably because it was felt that an association with the United Synagogue would be more likely to produce substantial material backing for the erection of the new Synagogue.

As yet, no site had been decided upon. Hilltop Road, West Hampstead, was considered, but the honorary officers of the St. John's Wood Synagogue in Abbey Road objected that this was too close to their place of worship. Eventually a site about half a mile further away was selected, on the corner of West End Lane and Dennington Park Road.

The well-known architect, Delissa Joseph, who was Bentwich's brother-in-law, was commissioned to design a Synagogue with its frontage in West End Lane. Joseph discussed his plans with his uncle, Hermann Adler, who was of the opinion that the Ark should be at the east or south-east end of the building. To comply with this view, Frank I. Lyons suggested turning the Synagogue round so that the frontage was in Dennington Park Road, and Delissa Joseph altered his plans accordingly. The proposals for the new Synagogue came before the Council of the United Synagogue in July, 1890, and it was resolved :

'That it is desirable to assist in the founding and erecting a Synagogue in the district of Hampstead, for persons of the Jewish religion who use the Polish or German ritual.'

It was also resolved to require from the committee of the proposed Synagogue the usual undertaking 'on behalf of the present and future congregation of that Synagogue, that such congregation will in all respects conform to, be bound by, carry out, and observe' the provisions of the deed of foundation and trust upon which the United Synagogue was based. The Council voted to advance a sum of £5,000 towards the building fund, provided a further £6,000 could be raised by voluntary contributions, and in order to strengthen the appeal for this amount Benjamin L. Cohen, one of the vice-presidents of the United Synagogue, agreed to become president of the Hampstead movement and Henry E. Beddington became treasurer of the building fund. The other honorary officers of the movement were at this stage Frank I. Lyons, chairman; Herbert Bentwich, vice-chairman; John Meredith, treasurer; and Samuel Moses, honorary secretary.

Canvassing of the district produced a large number of promises to join the Synagogue when it was built, and donations to the building fund soon amounted to £13,000, which included £5,000 advanced by the United Synagogue. To augment the funds still further a bazaar and fancy fair was held in the Great Hall of the Portman Rooms, Baker Street, in May, 1891. The daily newspapers described the bazaar in detail and the 'Jewish Chronicle' devoted a special supplement to it. At 3 o'clock on 5th May the bazaar was opened by Lady Rothschild. The stalls were organised by

19

the most prominent ladies of the community including Mrs. Hermann Adler; there were various sideshows, theatrical performances, and an elaborate refreshment saloon, and music was provided by the band of the Grenadier Guards and the Pompadour Ladies' Band.

The motif of the bazaar was 'A Street in Jerusalem' and, according to the 'Daily News', 'flitting figures that seemed to belong to far countries mingled with the throng and gave piquancy to a scene which was different from anything ever witnessed in London before.' A 'Book of the Fair' was issued, containing both a complete programme of the bazaar and original literary and artistic contributions from figures such as Israel Abrahams, Joseph Jacobs, Lady Magnus, Israel Zangwill and Solomon J. Solomon. Altogether over 6,000 people visited the bazaar and it excited an extraordinary amount of interest.

The bazaar committee's report in September, 1891, described the affair as 'a social, artistic and financial success without precedent in the Jewish community in London.' It is an accurate comment, indicative of the social status and fashionable tastes of the members of the 'Hampstead movement.'

CHAPTER II

The Events of 1892

ON 13TH MARCH, 1892, the feast of Purim, the foundation stone of the Synagogue was laid by Benjamin L. Cohen, vice-president of the United Synagogue. It was a unique ceremony in which, as a gesture of good will, 'to illustrate the unity of purpose which animated the several branches of the community,' Hermann Adler took part with the Haham (Dr. Gaster), the Rev. Simeon Singer of the New West End Synagogue and the Rev. Professor D. W. Marks of the West London Synagogue (Reform). 900 people attended the ceremony. The walls of the Synagogue were already up, but a tarpaulin was stretched over what would eventually be the roof, and the bleak winds which penetrated into the edifice caused some discomfort.

The daily papers made a special point of the musical arrangements for the service. Adler had refused to allow a mixed choir to take part in the ceremony, so the Rev. Francis L. Cohen of the Borough Synagogue, whom the Committee had asked to organise the musical part of the service, assembled an adult male choir of 23 voices accompanied by an orchestra of 23 instruments.[1] The Rev. S. Manné of the Dalston Synagogue officiated, and the music selected was mainly from Mendelssohn, though Psalm 100 was sung in Hebrew to the tune known as 'The Old Hundredth' and one of the compositions of the Rev. Marcus Hast of the Great Synagogue (Cohen's father-in-law) was included. The 'Jewish Chronicle' report of the ceremony gave this description of the building :

'The new Synagogue is situated in Dennington Park Road, West End Lane, and is arranged to accommodate 700 worshippers. The plan of the interior is based upon an octagon from which spring the ribs supporting the dome. The Ark is recessed from the South-east side of the octagon and grouped around the Ark are the reader's desk and the pulpit, raised to the level of the Ark platform and approached by handsome stairs. This grouping of Ark and Almemar at one end of the Synagogue, is new to London ... The facade is in red brick and red stone, and consists of a great central tower, flanked by wings containing the vestibules and by smaller towers enclosing the staircases. The style adopted is Romanesque ... The cost of the Synagogue and Schools to be attached to it will be about £11,000.'[2]

A few weeks after the laying of the foundation stone, the Committee proceeded to appoint officials for the new Synagogue. The Rev. S. Manné, who had officiated on 13th March, was interviewed in respect of the position of Reader of the Synagogue. He said that he had been Chazan at Fashion Street for eighteen months before going to Dalston in 1888, that he would take any steps that the Committee desired in order to improve his education, and that his debts did not exceed £50. He was willing to accept the office of Reader on the terms proposed by the Committee, and it was agreed to appoint him.

The Committee next met a week later, on 17th April, and offered the position of choirmaster to Algernon Lindo, who had been in charge of the choir for the Hampstead Sabbath afternoon services and who was a member of an old London Sephardi family. Lindo, asked whether he felt it would be feasible to have a purely voluntary choir, said that in his opinion a basis of professional voices was necessary, and suggested two sopranos, two altos, two tenors and two basses.

In due course Lindo went to see Hermann Adler about the consecration of the Synagogue, planned for September, and informed Adler that he was training a mixed choir for the occasion. Adler's reply, as on the occasion of the laying of the foundation stone, was that he had no objection to ladies singing in the congregation but he could not sanction their being in the choir. As a result, Lindo's choir did not sing at the consecration at all, and instead the male choir of the New West End Synagogue, augmented by male choristers from other Synagogues, and a small string orchestra, took part. However, a mixed choir sang at regular services from the first Sabbath the Synagogue was opened, and the Chief Rabbi tacitly accepted the situation.

The position of beadle went to Charles Abrahams, whose wife was to act as gallery attendant. Like many other beadles of the time, Abrahams was of Dutch-Jewish origin. He was given a detailed account of what was expected of him, and was informed that 'the Committee would act as judges of any disrespect he might shew to any member of the congregation'. He and his wife, among their other tasks, would also have to attend to the dead and dying. Despite his formidable list of duties, Abrahams served the congregation efficiently and loyally until he retired in 1930.

When it came to the appointment of a minister, there was little doubt as to the man whom the Committee would approach first. In fact, more than a year before, unofficial approaches had been made to the Rev. Morris Joseph to see if he would be interested in the appointment when the time came. Now, despite the fact that several applications were received in response to an advertisement in the 'Jewish Chronicle', Frank I. Lyons had a further unofficial interview with Morris Joseph.

Joseph stated that if he were invited to become the minister of the Hampstead Synagogue, he would be willing to put himself under the spiritual jurisdiction of the Chief Rabbi and to perform all the normal duties of a minister of the United Synagogue. He would not make alterations in the service without the approval of the Board of Management, but would insist on complete freedom of the pulpit. On 8th

May the honorary officers had a lengthy interview with Joseph, who again said that he would not consent to being muzzled in the pulpit or to avoid contentious matters in his sermons. He described his standpoint as 'liberal conservative Judaism', somewhere between orthodoxy and reform. (His position was later elaborated in his famous work, 'Judaism as Creed and Life', in which he referred to his views lying 'midway between the orthodoxy which regards the Shulchan Aruch, or at least the Talmud, as the final authority in Judaism, and the extreme liberalism which, setting little store by the historic sentiment as a factor of the Jewish consciousness, would lightly cut the religion loose from the bonds of Tradition.'³) Presumably because of his views about the restoration of sacrifices, he told the Committee that he did not wish it to be part of his duties to read prayers in the Synagogue, and Lyons said that this condition would be acceptable.

The committee, meeting on 10th May, decided to recommend that Morris Joseph be appointed, though Herbert Bentwich, A. J. Benjamin and A. Jacob abstained from voting. Now the proposal had to receive the approval of the Chief Rabbi, in accordance with normal United Synagogue practice. On 19th May, Adler replied that he could not give his sanction to the appointment. Urged to reconsider his decision, he had a meeting with Morris Joseph and on 27th May wrote to Frank Lyons in these terms:

'Dear Mr. Lyons,

In accordance with the request addressed to me by you and your colleagues, I had a long interview with the Rev. Morris Joseph yesterday.

You will remember having admitted to me at our recent interview that your Committee would not be justified in appointing a minister who in the event of being called upon to read any service or part of a service felt himself compelled to decline undertaking such duty. Mr. Joseph,

Herbert Bentwich, LL.B.

Frank I. Lyons – from an oil painting by Solomon J. Solomon, R.A.

The Synagogue choir, about 1900

when questioned by me on this point, stated that he could not conscientiously read any of the prayers in which supplication is offered up for the restoration of the sacrificial rite.

I also deemed it advisable to afford him the opportunity of explaining the religious views which he has embodied in various sermons which have been published in the "Jewish Chronicle". The explanations that he offered proved that I had been correct in my surmise that his opinions are not in accord with the teachings of traditional Judaism. These opinions, Mr. Joseph proceeded to state, he would have felt it his bounden duty to expound and to advocate, if appointed minister of the Hampstead Synagogue.

I have, therefore, to my keen regret, no alternative but to adhere to the determination which I communicated to your Honorary Secretary in my letter of the 19th inst., and to withhold my sanction of the appointment of Mr. Joseph as minister of the Hampstead Synagogue.

Kindly communicate this decision to your colleagues,

Believe me to be,
Yours very faithfully,
H. Adler.'

Now the storm of public controversy broke. The correspondence columns of the 'Jewish Chronicle' again resounded with the affairs of Hampstead. Morris Joseph himself wrote a letter to the paper in which he stated :

'The Chief Rabbi declares me unfit for the ministry of one of his Synagogues; *first,* because I have sanctioned the use of instrumental music at my Sabbath Afternoon services; *secondly,* because I have publicly expressed a disbelief in the future revival of sacrifices, such disbelief being, in the judgment of the Chief Rabbi, opposed to the teachings of Scripture; and *thirdly,* because in several sermons ... I have published views "at variance with traditional Judaism". This is the head and front of my offending ...

c

I have long felt . . . that progress, with its attendant salvation for English Judaism, is impossible within the confines of the Synagogue as by Rabbinical law established . . . All that has to be considered is whether the religious needs of a progressive congregation are to be ignored and its spiritual life starved, in obedience to a rigid system; or whether the time has not come for identifying the Synagogue with that catholic spirit and policy, which while duly respecting the opinions of conservative minds, will give full satisfaction to liberal aspiration.'[4]

The 'Chronicle' itself commented on this letter that it told 'in words, the moderation of which but increases their effect, that the United Synagogue has no room for men like the Rev. Morris Joseph, to preach righteousness in the great congregation.'

Solomon Schechter, now living in Cambridge, expressed his deep disquiet that this had to be the state of affairs in Anglo-Jewry. He pointed out that if doctrines were to become the test of a minister, then the greatest names in Jewish learning – Zunz, Graetz, Herzfeld, Joel, Gotthold Salomon, Rapaport and others – would never have been permitted to preach in a United Synagogue. If there had to be a test, it should be one of learning and scholarship: 'And so I should like also to plead to allow doctrine to rest quiet; for an appeal to it will only breed cant and hypocrisy. If a test there be, and it is most desirable that there should be one, let it be a thorough knowledge of the Bible and of the Talmud as well as the Posekim, a thorough acquaintance with Jewish history and a sound secular education.'

But notwithstanding the number of Joseph's supporters who were bitterly disappointed by the Chief Rabbi's decision, Joseph had no alternative but to write to the honorary secretary of the congregation on 29th May, 'that, being anxious to take the course that would best promote the convenience of the committee, he withdrew his acceptance of the invitation by which the committee had asked him to be the minister of the Hampstead Synagogue.' The following year, Joseph succeeded Professor Marks at the West London Synagogue, eventually retiring from office in 1921.[5] A friendly connection was, however, henceforth always maintained between Morris Joseph and Hampstead.

The Hampstead Committee carefully considered the applications which had been put to one side in the hope that Joseph would get the appointment, their choice eventually lying between A. A. Green and J. F. Stern. After a long discussion it was decided to send a telegram to Green in Sunderland, inviting him to preach in London, and if this could not be arranged, then a delegation of three members of the Committee, Lyons, Bentwich and Meredith, would go to Sunderland to hear him preach at his own Synagogue. Green replied that he was prepared to come to London, and after a meeting with the Hampstead Committee on 30th June he gave a sermon at the St. John's Wood Synagogue on 9th July. The committee met again the following day, when Green was elected minister and secretary.

His farewell sermon was preached in Sunderland on 13th August, and the Sunderland 'Daily Echo', in its issue of that date, published a photograph of him with an appreciative account of his work in the town. The congregation presented him with an illuminated address and a library of 66 books, and the children gave him a reading lamp, an inkstand and another illuminated address. He took up his duties in Hampstead at the beginning of September, and participated in the consecration of the Synagogue on Sunday afternoon, 18th September, with the Chief Rabbi and the Rev. S. Manné.

In the meantime, the question of ritual reform was very much to the fore again. Faced with a mounting number of requests for modification, Lord Rothschild, the president of the United Synagogue, had discussed the matter with Hermann Adler in the interval between the death of his father and his own appointment as Chief Rabbi. It was agreed that there should be a recognised procedure to deal with proposed reforms and a recommendation was adopted which stated that :

'Whenever a question shall be raised by the Board of Management or Committee of a Metropolitan or Provincial Synagogue contributing to the support of the office of Chief Rabbi as to any proposed alteration to the form of worship or ritual thereat, the Chief Rabbi shall consult upon such question with a Committee to be convened by him, and to consist of the preachers of such contributing synagogues, unless he shall deem it proper to authorise such alteration without consultation with the proposed Committee.'

Several Synagogues now took the opportunity of presenting their views. In Hampstead, discussion on the details of the ritual had been deferred in accordance with the decision reached at the critical meeting on 10th November, 1889, until the Synagogue had been built. The time had now come when the matter had to be resolved once and for all. On 28th February, 1892, the Hampstead Committee unanimously carried a resolution moved by Frank I. Lyons and seconded by Herbert Bentwich :

'That the honorary officers be authorised to present to the Chief Rabbi the original programme of an improved service which was submitted to the late Chief Rabbi, with power to take any further steps they might think necessary for procuring the adoption of such programme.'

At the same time the Borough, Central and New West End Synagogues also submitted suggestions, though only after long and bitter meetings of their own members at which wide divergences of opinion were expressed. Common to almost all was the wish to discontinue the repetition of the *Amidah,* particularly at the Musaph service, with its references to the restoration of sacrifices. There was also considerable support for the discontinuance of the *duchan* ceremony on festivals – both points refused by Nathan Marcus Adler on more than one occasion.

The Chief Rabbi convened a conference of preachers in May, 1892. The meetings lasted over four days, with Dr. Adler in the chair and Simeon Singer as honorary secretary. Almost all the proposed changes were bitterly opposed by Rabbi Dr. Lerner of the Federation of Synagogues, but frequently the views of what one observer called 'the "Young England" party among the ministers' prevailed. At first the majority opposed the non-repetition of the *Amidah,* but after 'a most earnest and learned speech' by Singer the majority decided that, while the *Amidah* must be repeated at Shacharith, at the Musaph service the repetition could be dispensed with.

Hermann Adler had already informed the Hampstead congregation in 1889 that 'As to the *Amidah,* its repetition in the service was not vital to Judaism'. His authoritative statement of the decisions of the conference was made public the 'Jewish Chronicle' on 17th June. 'The following principle,' he stated, 'has guided me in my decisions. I have given my sanction to those alterations which do not violate any statute (*din*) of traditional Judaism, and which do not affect our statutory liturgy . . . It was represented to me that these alterations were calculated to enhance the impressiveness of your services, and to rouse and preserve the devotion of your worshippers.' He confirmed the decision to permit the non-repetition of the *Amidah,* basing himself on the precedent of the Spanish and Portuguese congregations of London and Amsterdam, whose orthodoxy was unquestioned.[6]

But despite the support which many of the ministers present at the conference had given to the proposal to eliminate *duchaning,* Dr. Adler stated that: 'The sacred rite of *birkath kohanim* must be preserved . . . I grieve to learn that in some congregations the practice of this rite has been permitted to

29

fall into abeyance.' However, in 1889 he had told the representatives of Hampstead that 'It was in the power of the Committee of the Synagogue, after its establishment, to make alterations in the method of the recital of the blessings of the *Kohanim,* subject to an appeal by any member of the congregation to the Chief Rabbi', and it was on the basis of this tacit concession that the Hampstead committee decided that the priestly blessing would be read on festivals by the chazan and not bythe *kohanim.*

On the whole the congregations which had put forward proposals were satisfied. The annual report of the New West End, for example, in 1892 stated: 'It is gratifying to be able to report that the greater part of the demands put forward by our Congregation were approved by the Conference, and many of them were ultimately sanctioned by the Chief Rabbi.'

Some other Synagogues now considered whether to adopt some or all of the Chief Rabbi's concessions. The Board of Management at Bayswater sent members of their congregation a circular inviting views on a long list of proposed changes, including the non-repetition of the *Amidah.* The circular aroused strong feelings of opposition on the part of an influential section of members, some of whose replies were harshly critical of the proposals. In the end a further circular was sent out in which only the mildest of the original proposals were put forward and the more radical, including any reference to the *Amidah,* were omitted. Hermann Adler, who had been preacher at Bayswater from 1864 to 1891, expressed his satisfaction that his old congregation had maintained its reputation for orthodoxy by not adopting any fundamental changes.

Even congregations as far away as Australia heard strong echoes of the controversies in London, and many of the modifications introduced in Hampstead and the New West End were introduced there. (The example of Hampstead and some other Synagogues was also followed a little later in another respect, when a number of colonial congregations decided that if a mixed choir could sing at Hampstead, which was under the Chief Rabbi's jurisdiction, they could permit themselves the same concession.) As they came into existence, some new congregations at once proceeded to use a form of worship based on Hermann Adler's concessions, though in some cases there later came a return to the traditional form of service. In Brondesbury, for example, the repetition of the *Amidah* was reintroduced in 1911 and *duchaning* in 1912, in deference to the wishes of the minister, Dayan H. M. Lazarus, and in 1935 a movement in favour of a mixed choir was defeated by the strong opposition of Dayan Lazarus.

As far as Hampstead was concerned, a Ritual Sub-Committee met several times in September, 1892, to consider the Sabbath and festival services in the light of the Chief Rabbi's decisions, and advantage was taken of the various concessions which had been made.[7]

The provisional committee remained in office until December, 1892, when an election was held under the rules of the United Synagogue. Those elected were: Wardens – Frank I. Lyons and Herbert Bentwich; representatives at United Synagogue Council – John Meredith (financial representative), Alexander Jacob and Samuel Moses; Board of Management – Arthur J. Benjamin, Maurice Davis, J. J. Duveen, M. Eilenberg, C. Marcus, Henry Nathan, S. Pizer, Bernard Solomon, David Solomon and George Vandamm.

The relatives of Herbert Bentwich were particularly prominent both on the new board and in the membership of the congregation. Bernard and David Solomon were brothers of the artist, Solomon J. Solomon, who lived in St. John's Wood and worshipped at Hampstead. One of their sisters, Susie, was Herbert Bentwich's wife, and another, Lily, an artist in her own right, had married Delissa Joseph, who had designed the Synagogue.

Delissa Joseph himself did not live in the district, but in Holland Road, West Kensington, and had been one of the

31

founders as well as the architect of the Hammersmith Synagogue erected in 1890. (His original design for Hammersmith differed from that for Hampstead in that the *bimah* was in the centre of the building, but in the course of alterations completed in 1896 it was moved to the position immediately in front of the Ark which Joseph had adopted in Hampstead.)[8]

Many of the Solomon family were living in Hampstead and St. John's Wood and two rows of seats in the ladies' gallery at Hampstead were specifically reserved for female members of the family. Solomon J. Solomon had willingly assisted with artistic advice both on the occasion of the bazaar at the Portman Rooms, where the motif of 'A Street in Jerusalem' was based on his design and one of his pictures was raffled in aid of the building fund, and in the erection of the Synagogue. He designed a set of stained-glass windows depicting the Biblical story of the creation, though he was not completely satisfied with the result and some criticised the pictures as offending against orthodox tradition.[9]

Other distinguished early members of the congregation included Joseph Jacobs, the historian and folklorist, who went to the United States in 1900 as revising editor of the 'Jewish Encyclopaedia'.

The opening of the Synagogue brought about a rapid increase in membership. By the end of 1892 there were 293 seats let in the Synagogue, and several other congregations were suffering the loss of members who found Hampstead more accessible. By the end of 1899 the number of seats let was 668 (366 in the body of the Synagogue and 302 in the gallery), and the membership continued to increase until Hampstead was the largest congregation within the United Synagogue.

In their annual reports to the congregation in these years, the honorary officers expressed pleasure at the success of the new Synagogue. In the 1894 report they stated, 'The Honorary Officers do not confine their solicitude ... to their natural desire to increase the Member Roll of the Congregation, but they are desirous also that the Synagogue, with its dignified and impressive services, may be the means of winning recruits for the larger Congregation of Israel, instilling a love for Jewish traditions in the hearts of the rising generation, and bringing as many as possible, through the Synagogue, into touch with the charitable work of the community.'

The following year they reported that 'the number of Jewish residents in the neighbourhood is increasing very rapidly', and as a consequence of the steady rise in the number of members of the Synagogue, the seating accommodation gradually became inadequate. At first the interior of the building had been arranged with seats around the sides only, the centre being left empty, but now seats were placed in the centre to cope with the increasing membership. In 1897, to mark Queen Victoria's diamond jubilee, a classroom building was erected at the side of the Synagogue, providing a board room and *sukkah,* as well as classrooms. Frank I. Lyons laid the foundation stone, and the building was consecrated by the Chief Rabbi.

In 1900, plans drawn up by Delissa Joseph for the further extension of the Synagogue were approved, and the board expressed their confidence that the result would be 'the transformation of the already handsome Synagogue into one of the finest and most commodious in England.' The work was completed in 1901 and had the effect of considerably increasing seating accommodation, particularly in the ladies' gallery.[10]

The honorary officers and board were pleased with their efforts; but it was otherwise with Herbert Bentwich. He was not prepared to congratulate himself on the way his dream of a revival of Judaism based on Hampstead had been translated into reality. As early as May, 1893, he complained that the most elementary test of the well-being of a Synagogue was personal attendance at services by the members, and by

33

this test Hampstead was not a great success. Norman Bentwich has stated :

'My Father's satisfaction was short-lived. Instead of a religious revival in Hampstead, the place became a Mecca of good-tempered respectability: plenty of response to charitable appeals, thronged congregations on the high days and holydays: but the Finchley Road was crowded with Jewish shoppers on the Sabbath. From my Father's point of view – "Ye shall be unto me a kingdom of priests and a holy nation" – in his understanding of those words, the synagogue was a failure. It could not be otherwise. After two years of office as Warden, he was not re-elected. He retreated to a small pew, whence he could survey the congregation without mixing with it. Yet such was the demand for seating accommodation that within a few years the synagogue had to be widely extended; and when, in the extension, his pew was removed, he made it the occasion for discontinuing his membership.'[11]

Writing to A. A. Green, Bentwich gave vent to his severe disappointment that Hampstead had 'surrendered most of the ideals with which the Hampstead movement was first associated' and had 'chosen to displace the originator of the movement in which the ideal held so large a place. Alas for our ideals!' In 1915 Bentwich, who had given the Synagogue its *ner tamid*, offered to present a stained-glass window to mark his association with the congregation, but it was felt that the design he had in mind would need to be changed to fit in with other plans for the alteration of the Synagogue, and Bentwich withdrew his offer. Henceforward, Bentwich's country home in Kent, designed by Delissa Joseph and with its own synagogue, was to be his sanctuary, where his ideals would rule.

34

CHAPTER III

The Form of Worship at Hampstead

THE MAIN LITURGICAL principles which arose out of all the controversies of the early years have, on the whole, been maintained with, as we shall see, only one important change. Ritual reform remained a live issue in the community throughout the first decade of the Synagogue's existence, and attempts were made to secure still further concessions for a number of congregations. But the issue gradually developed from one concerned merely with an attitude to the liturgy to one of much wider significance – the attitude to Jewish practice and the authority of the Bible in general.

Hampstead, with its compromise form of service, did not go far enough for those who wanted change.[1] On several notable earlier occasions this had already been made quite clear. This first was the resignation of the eight committee members who in 1889 could not accept the limitations which the Chief Rabbi's ecclesiastical jurisdiction involved. A second occasion was the rejection of the Rev. Morris Joseph, with all that it implied.

The year 1892, in which the Synagogue was opened, saw another event of far-reaching significance with the publication of Claude Goldsmid Montefiore's Hibbert Lectures on 'The Origin and Growth of Religion as Illustrated by the Religion of the Ancient Hebrews'. In these lectures, Montefiore presented a view of the Bible which to the comfortable, complacent Anglo-Jewish community of the 1890's, was revolutionary and iconoclastic. All, he said, was not

35

Divine and binding. The findings of modern Bible criticism could not be brushed aside. Judaism had to be understood against its historical background, and religious rites and institutions which suited one historical era were not necessarily in harmony with another era.

The implications of these views led logically towards something far more radical than the merely liturgical modifications with which Hampstead was flirting, and also went further than the views of Morris Joseph, who regarded the conclusions of the Bible critics as 'strictly contentious matter, . . . far from being generally accepted by Biblical scholars.'

While Montefiore's ideas were being discussed in the community, further attempts at liturgical reform were still being made in Hampstead and elsewhere. In 1895, for example, a referendum of Hampstead members resulted in 113 of them voting in favour of introducing an organ into the Sabbath services, and 67 opposing it. In 1889 the provisional committee had felt it would be 'inexpedient at the present time' to have an organ. This new proposal was likewise not put into effect.

At the annual meeting of the congregation in 1898, Leopold J. Greenberg – whom Herzl called 'the most able of all my helpers' and who later became editor of the 'Jewish Chronicle' – suggested that a conference of ministers should be convened along the lines of that held in 1892, to consider a revision of the Sabbath and Festival services in order 'to make their services a living means of worship, and not to retain them as a sort of archaeological curiosity, all the funny little points of which must be preserved for the sake of antiquarian interest.'

It is probable, however, that at this stage at least, Greenberg was not thinking of anything more radical than a reorganisation of the service so that the Shacharith, which was more important and more beautiful than Musaph, could become the principal service. (A. A. Green, with his customary wit, made a similar plea for the Shacharith some four years later, when he said that some of the passages in it were incomparably beautiful, yet they were all said in the earlier part of the service and one had either to be a *minyan* man or a mourner to hear them – that was to say, in the case of an ordinary layman, he had either to lose his money or his father!)

In 1901 the Hon. Lily Montagu, who had been thinking along lines similar to those of Claude Montefiore, wrote an article in the 'Jewish Quarterly Review' on 'The Spiritual Possibilities of Judaism Today', not intending at first to propagate a new theology but to win back for Judaism those who were drifting away from it. As a result, a small committee was set up to plan special services, both for children and for adults, and in the beginning the idea was that these services would be supplementary to the existing Synagogue services. While there was some support, the movement was not taken too seriously. A. A. Green was a member of the committee, and it was he and Morris Joseph who suggested that the movement should be called the Jewish Religious Union. Other orthodox ministers like Simeon Singer of the New West End Synagogue and J. F. Stern of East London also associated themselves with its work.

In March, 1902, an approach was made to Hermann Adler asking him to allow the Union the use of United Synagogue premises for its services. Dr. Adler refused and made it clear that he was not in sympathy with the aims of the movement. The reason for his attitude soon became evident when Claude Montefiore stated publicly that he and his supporters in the Union did not accept the literal interpretation of the Bible and even questioned the scriptural account of the giving of the Ten Commandments.

A. A. Green had not objected to the use of the organ, the seating of the sexes together and the reading of prayers in English at the Union's services, but the tendency which was developing in the Union was to go beyond these points, and he and his orthodox colleagues were under some pressure to

37

withdraw. Eventually, in October, 1902, he made a statement to the Committee disagreeing with their action in placing themselves in opposition to the orthodox tradition, and stating in particular that, while he approved of changes in the external forms of worship so long as these were confined to non-statutory services, he could not support them if they were to be applied to the Sabbath services inside the Synagogue.

By the time of the committee meeting in November he had sent in a letter of resignation, and early in 1903 Singer and Stern also withdrew. The movement now embarked upon an independent path, under the leadership of Lily Montagu, Claude Montefiore and Israel Abrahams, and later developed into the Liberal Jewish Synagogue.[2]

In later years A. A. Green said that he regarded the predominantly English service of the Liberal Synagogue as 'an emasculation' and impromptu English prayers as 'the worst kind of *chukkath hagoyim*'. Solomon Schechter, by now living in America, was bitterly disappointed at the nature of the movement which his former pupil Montefiore had initiated: 'What the whole thing means,' he said, 'is not liberal Judaism, but liberal Christianity.'

At much the same period there was yet another attempt in Hampstead itself at devising a further scheme for ritual reform, not involving any controversial points of theology as such. At the annual general meeting in May, 1902, Max Herz (who was a leading member of the Jewish Religious Union) moved, 'That a meeting shall be called within four weeks to discuss the question of what could be done in order to attract more Jews in Hampstead, who do not now participate in Jewish communal life; that such meeting be open to non-members of the Synagogue, and that the committee be asked to make the meeting and its object well known.'

In June a public meeting was held on the subject and it was decided that as the Jewish Religious Union had just been formed the best course would be to wait and see what the Union was going to do. By November, A. A. Green had withdrawn his support from the Union, and a further meeting was held at Hampstead on 30th November.

S. Alexander proposed, 'That a committee be appointed to consider and report as to the advisability of introducing certain modifications in the synagogue services', stating that while he desired changes in the services, he was 'dead against radical reform'. In supporting him, Green explained why he had resigned from the Jewish Religious Union, and said: 'I have left them because I differed from them in a point of principle, but I never in my life was associated with men whom I respected more, with men whose ideas were evidently more single-minded and had but one aim, and that to do good. They may be mistaken. I believe their course is a mistaken one at the present moment...' Alexander's resolution was carried unanimously and a sub-committee was set up, with Samuel Moses as chairman and Leopold Greenberg as honorary secretary, to formulate proposals for ritual reform.

After deliberations lasting nearly a year the committee produced its report. Among other points, it suggested replacing the divided service on Sabbaths and Festivals, with its resultant meagre attendance at Shacharith, by a continuous service combining the most attractive features of both Shacharith and Musaph, with an abbreviated reading from the Torah, and with a greater use of English. The board of management rejected the shortening of the reading of the Torah on the casting vote of the chairman, but accepted the other points, provided the whole service took no more than two hours. A rehearsal was held in the Synagogue one evening, but it was found to be impossible to conduct the proposed service with proper devotion within anything like the time limit set by the board.

The committee then turned its attention to the Friday evening service, and produced a plan for a service com-

39

mencing at 6.45 p.m. throughout the year, lasting no more than one hour, and including a sermon or Bible reading, some English prayers, and the participation of the choir. The board of management agreed to the plan, and the Chief Rabbi gave his consent. The first service along these lines was held on 4th December, 1903, with nearly 200 people present. At the second service a large falling-off in attendance was noticeable, and the numbers continually decreased until after eight weeks the experiment was abandoned.

The second days of Festivals

From that time onwards, little has been attempted at Hampstead in the way of large-scale alteration of the ritual, though from time to time some specific issues have come to the fore. One example is the question of the observance of the second days of the Festivals. This had aroused bitter controversy in the time of Nathan Marcus Adler, and it was an idea which had exercised the minds of the founders of the congregation, for they had felt it necessary to make a recommendation that 'the Synagogue will be open for service on the second days of the Holydays'.

The attendances on those days must have been poor in the early period, leading the board of management to decide in November, 1894, 'That on the second days of the festivals, the morning service shall commence at 8.30 and be continued without interval until completion'. This suggests that the attendance was not large enough to justify dividing the service into two. For many years the attendances were meagre, though this resolution is no longer in effect, and it is only in post-war years that an improvement has been evident.

Soon after the establishment of the State of Israel in 1948, the abolition of the second days was raised again. At the annual meeting in 1949 it was suggested that the Chief Rabbi should be asked to establish uniformity in the observance of the Festivals as in Israel, where the second days of Pesach,

40

Samuel Alman, A.R.C.M.

The Rev. Wolf Stoloff

Henry Gledhill – from an oil painting by Hermann Fechenbach

Samuel Moses, M.A. – from an oil painting by M. D. Alston

Shavuoth and Sukkoth have never been observed. It was also suggested that there would probably be larger attendances at the Synagogue if only one day were kept, but there was strong criticism of the idea from a number of members, and the proposal was not proceeded with.

The Israeli pronunciation

At the same meeting, it was decided to ask the Chief Rabbi to arrange for suitable parts of the service to be read in the Israeli pronunciation and for this to be the pronunciation used in the Hebrew classes. In accordance with this decision, the *Sidra* was henceforth read in the Israeli pronunciation at Hampstead.

At the annual meeting in 1952 Sydney Goldberg moved a motion advocating a return to the use of the Ashkenazi pronunciation. Mark Kleiner, the chairman, said he had been advised that this motion could not be accepted, because the original decision of 1949 was out of order, since it did not comply with the by-laws of the United Synagogue, the Deed of Foundation and Trust or the Act of Parliament governing the United Synagogue. His ruling was, therefore, that the decision taken in 1949 had to be rescinded and the pronunciation used in the Hampstead Synagogue had to be Ashkenazi, in accordance with the laws of the United Synagogue.

A lengthy discussion followed, in which several voices called this a retrograde step which went against the strong feelings of many of the congregation. It also went against the strong feelings of the Rev. I. Levy, who expressed his complete dis-approval of Mr. Kleiner's action at a meeting of the board of management, stating that though the United Synagogue maintained the Ashkenazi ritual, he did not believe that ritual involved matters of pronunciation. He declared some time later that he could not forgive the Zionist movement for having failed to support the initiative that had been shown in Hampstead in 1949 and having thus missed a great opportunity to introduce 'the real pronunciation of Hebrew' into the classes and synagogues.

In July, 1962, the Chief Rabbi communicated a ruling on the subject to the President of the United Synagogue. He said that in 1952 he had not felt justified in permitting a sudden switch over to the Israeli pronunciation on *halachic* and pedagogic grounds. The change had to come about as the result of the gradual expansion of spoken, modern Hebrew in the community. Basing himself on subsequent educational trends, however, he had now decided to allow day schools and Hebrew classes to use the Israeli pronunciation provided teachers had received adequate preliminary guidance. For the present the Ashkenazi pronunciation had to be retained in the Synagogue service except for the prayer for the State of Israel and the reading of a Bar Mitzvah portion. The Hampstead classes immediately changed over to the Israeli pronunciation. In a survey of the opinions of ministers, published in the 'Jewish Chronicle' in June, 1965, the Rev. Raymond Apple said that if there were any possibility of introducing the Israeli pronunciation into the Synagogue he would be in favour.

The great 'duchaning' controversy

One of the points of ritual on which Hermann Adler gave way to the founders of the Synagogue was the omission of the ceremonial recital of the Priestly Blessing on festivals. Adler stated that 'it was in the power of the Committee of the Synagogue, after its establishment, to make alterations in the method of the recital of the blessings of the *Kohanim*, subject to an appeal by any member of the Congregation to the Chief Rabbi.'

The Committee decided that 'the blessings of the Priests will on Festivals be read by the Minister' in exactly the same manner as on Sabbaths, without the *Kohanim* raising their hands in the traditional fashion and pronouncing the blessing word for word. The fear which motivated the Committee was presumably the possible effect of the ceremony on the decorum of the service, and their disapproval of the character of some of the *Kohanim* who might take part.

But throughout a period spanning almost half a century, a campaign was waged by Elsley Zeitlyn, a noted communal worker who was himself a *Kohen,* to have the ceremony restored to the service. At general meetings in 1913, 1914, 1927, 1938, 1954, and 1955 he put his case. On the first occasion, the chairman, Emil Kahn, ruled Zeitlyn's motion out of order. By the next year, Zeitlyn had changed the wording of his motion and put it forward once again. This time there was considerable debate but the motion was narrowly defeated by 18 votes to 16.

In 1927 Zeitlyn tried again. He said that it was irrelevant to introduce the fitness or unfitness of those who would pronounce the blessing. By such a standard very few people would be found fit to discharge any of the offices of the Synagogue and few even of the characters in the Bible would pass such a test. In any case, a natural sense of self-restraint would hold back those who felt themselves unfitted from performing the office, and perhaps participation in the ceremony would have a good effect upon some whose lives fell short of a high moral standard. The Biblical command to pronounce the benediction imposed no test of fitness, as the blessing was God's and not that of the person who pronounced it, and the obligation rested upon all *kohanim.*

But a number of members argued that the motion was a retrograde step which would spoil the dignity of the service and bring discord into the congregation. It was claimed that Zeitlyn was carrying on a one-man campaign and that there was no real demand among the members for the restoration of *duchaning.* Both Hermann Adler, who was a *kohen,* and J. H. Hertz had attended festival services at Hampstead and had not objected to the mode of service as it stood. 23 members voted for the motion, but a large majority opposed it.

43

Eleven years later, in 1938, Zeitlyn submitted a similar resolution. He said he could not acquiesce in a state of affairs which he considered wrong. He had raised the matter at that stage particularly hoping that, in the interval since 1927, 'other influences and other guidance would have come forward.' He was doubtlessly referring to the fact that the minister of the congregation was now Dayan Gollop, a member of the London Beth Din. But once more only a few voices supported him, and the vast majority agreed with John Lewis, who said there was no widespread desire to alter 'the devout and decorous service' which had become customary at Hampstead. The founders of the Synagogue had wanted a modified service and only on that condition had they agreed to join the United Synagogue. If Hampstead now adopted *duchaning* they would have to do away with their mixed choir and resume repetition of the Musaph *Amidah*. Once again Zeitlyn was heavily defeated.

The next attempt was made in 1954. Zeitlyn pointed out that Hampstead was the only constituent of the United Synagogue where *duchaning* was not practised. He had been told that it was a tradition at Hampstead not to *duchan,* but a custom could not be established on a breach of the law. In support of Zeitlyn, Israel Finestein argued that Hermann Adler had consented to modifications in the service only because of the particular circumstances of the time, but the community had changed since then and those circumstances no longer applied. But again the motion was defeated, by 18 votes to 15. Zeitlyn tried once more the following year. Henry Gledhill, in opposing the motion, said that its sponsor had tried and tried and tried again but he was confident that the congregation would once again turn down the proposal. They did, by 29 votes to 23.

Yet by Rosh Hashanah, a few months later, there was *duchaning* at Hampstead. Press reports of the meeting in May had led to the matter being ventilated throughout the Jewish community. On 8th June the Chief Rabbi, Dr. Israel

Brodie, wrote to the secretary of the United Synagogue and categorically ruled that 'any *Kohen* present who wishes to do so be permitted to pronounce the Priestly Blessing during Divine Service at the Hampstead Synagogue on all occasions when it is the English *Minhag* to do so.' A few days later, the Hon. Ewen E. S. Montagu, president of the United Synagogue, made a statement to the United Synagogue Council in which he referred to the Chief Rabbi's ruling and said that in future it would be incumbent on the Hampstead Synagogue to conform to this ruling.

CHAPTER IV

A. A. Green

THE CONGREGATION WERE denied Morris Joseph in 1892, but though in a sense this made A. A. Green a second choice it was one they never regretted. For nearly forty years Green and the congregation worked in harmonious partnership. The two became almost synonymous. Green had the genius to translate into terms of practical possibility a very large part of the ideals which motivated the founders of the Synagogue, and he in his turn widened and deepened the scope of those ideals by his preaching and teaching and his personal example.

Aaron Asher Green was born in Goodman's Fields in East London on 18th September, 1860, the only son of Asher Green. His was a family that already had a long tradition of association with the ministry. His uncle was the Rev. Aaron Levy Green (1821–1883) of the Central Synagogue, who was one of the earliest members of the ministry to preach regularly in English, developing in his sermons and writings a reputation as something of a religious radical.

The Green family also had longstanding connections with the Great Synagogue in Duke's Place. A. A. Green as a boy of nine joined its choir, which was then under the direction of J. L. Mombach (1813–1880), who had a dominating influence on Synagogue music in this country. Green's membership of his choir gave him the opportunity of using his vocal gifts to good advantage as a soloist. It also made him expert in the ritual traditions of 'The Great', a training that was invaluable when it came to laying proper foundations for the service at Hampstead, where he was known to be meticulous in Synagogue procedure, and the slightest

46

deviation from *Minhag* would arouse his anger.

He was a keen student of Hebrew from his childhood. At the age of eight he was allowed to read the *Haphtarah* in Synagogue, and he taught other boys their Bar Mitzvah portions before he was Bar Mitzvah himself. In 1868 he entered the preparatory school of Jews' College, of which his uncle, A. L. Green, was honorary secretary. (The libraries of both A. L. and A. A. Green were subsequently presented to the College and today form part of its extensive library).[1] The College school was intended to provide an English and Hebrew education for 'the sons of our middle ranks', and Green remained a pupil there until he entered the College proper in 1876 to train for the ministry. The previous year he had been one of five pupils who edited a short-lived magazine called 'The Jews' College Journal'.

He dearly wanted to crown his Jews' College career by taking a degree, but before this could be achieved the need to earn a living became urgent, and he commenced work as a Hebrew teacher at the Stepney Jewish School and the Settles Street Hebrew Classes.

He spent all the time he could spare in study, and the encouragement he received from Michael Friedländer, principal of Jews' College, is acknowledged in Green's edition of the Passover Haggadah (first published in 1897). In his preface he paid tribute to Friedländer who had, he said, 'many years ago ... accompanied me to the British Museum to assist me in perusing the manuscripts.'

Green would not have claimed to be a great or original scholar, but from these early days onwards he prepared a number of papers, mostly on literary and historical subjects. He lectured to the Jews' College literary and debating society on the life and writings of Kalir, the medieval Hebrew poet, and on Jeremiah the prophet. He had an article in the jubilee supplement of the 'Jewish Chronicle' in 1891, entitled 'At the "King's Head" ', and his other historical papers included 'Old Purim Fair' ('Jewish Chronicle', 28th February,

1896) and 'The Exeter Hebrew Congregation: the Dead Communities of the West Country' ('J.C.', 25th March, 1910). His edition of the Haggadah, with translation, introduction and commentary, went through three editions.[2]

He was a candidate for the pulpit at the Central Synagogue on his uncle's death in 1883, but his youth and inexperience told against him. His first position was in Sheffield, where he married Miss Ada Jacob. His salary there was £150, of which £100 came from the Provincial Jewish Ministers' Fund, of which Green himself later became honorary secretary and vice-president.

From Sheffield he moved to Sunderland, where he remained from 1888 to 1892. In his 'History of the Sunderland Jewish Community, 1755–1955', Arnold Levy writes: 'With the advent of Mr. Green as minister things communally began to move swiftly. Never before had the Sunderland Jewish Community known such activity as during the few years of Mr. Green's ministry.'

Many of the Jews of Sunderland had come from Krottingen, near Kovno, and on the second day of Shavuoth, 1889, the whole of Krottingen was gutted by fire. When the news of the tragedy reached Sunderland a relief fund was immediately started, and A. A. Green was sent to Krottingen to organise the distribution of relief. When he returned to England he sent a detailed description to the 'Jewish Chronicle', which was published on 26th July, 1889, appealing for wider communal support for the relief fund.

But despite all his efforts for the immigrants, Green was rather too anglicised for their liking and this undoubtedly contributed to a final split in the Sunderland community, resulting, as in so many other long-settled communities faced with a wave of immigration, in the development of separate 'English' and 'foreign' congregations. In any case, as Arnold Levy remarks, it was evident that a small provincial community could not hold A. A. Green.

He was unsuccessful in his application for the position at

Bayswater which Hermann Adler vacated when he became Chief Rabbi in 1891 – the Rev. (later Rabbi Sir) Hermann Gollancz received the appointment – but Green was elected first minister of the Hampstead Synagogue. The eight years he had spent in the provinces were among the most important in his life. They gave him experience, even if for want of senior colleagues to advise and guide him, it was often that of trial and error. Later, as doyen of his profession, he pleaded the case of the provincial ministers, whom he called the heroes of the ministry. He appealed for adequate stipends and a scheme of professional guidance for them, and felt that instead of provincial congregations being just stepping-stones, they ought to become 'the goal of the best men we can produce.'

In 1892 he came to Hampstead, and Hampstead now became his life's work. A former pupil wrote of him, 'It was a happy union, both for Minister and congregants. Mr. Green was an ideal pastor. He loved his flock and his flock loved him. He was their counsellor, their guide and their devoted friend. In joy and in sorrow, in sickness and in health, he was ever at their service. A sad tale of illness would bring him in daily visits to the bedside, yet his work among his congregants did not prevent him from engaging energetically in social activities, both within and without the Jewish community.'

His ministry was a pastorate in a sense that Anglo-Jewry has made peculiarly its own. Green was the acknowledged representative figure of this type of ministry at its most classical, with its emphasis on preaching, teaching, pastoral work and acting as an ambassador of Jewry to the outside world. Green's concept of the ministry was given expression in his dedicatory sermon at the Conference of Anglo-Jewish Preachers in 1923, when he said :

'This Jewish ministry of which we are the component parts and of which we are so proud is not only new to this com-

49

munity, but it is something new in Judaism. If we examine its origin and understand its inner meaning, however greatly such a ministry as ours has ultimately justified itself, its necessity originally arose not as a sign of strength and growth in Jewish feeling, but as a sign of recognisable weakness and decadence ... Our chance and that of our successors lies in one direction alone, and that is in the force of character which inspires the mission of each of us and in the pious humility and religious self-sacrifice that, to our credit and to our pride, we recognise as so consistent a feature of the work of our colleagues in our great and honoured calling.'

Green believed strongly in the well-to-do Jews of the West taking responsibility for the welfare of those less well endowed in the East. He personally carried out and organised considerable welfare work in the East End, and deliberately involved his Hampstead congregants in his efforts.[3] For a number of years Green was chairman of the Soldiers' and Sailors' Dependants' Committee set up in the East End after the first World War. He served as a manager of various schools, took a serious interest in the Hampstead branch of the League of Nations Union, and was a frequent and popular lecturer on Judaism to Christian groups.

As early as the years of his provincial ministry, he had made inter-faith work one of his main interests. Arnold Levy records that after Green had lectured to a Christian group on 'Jewish Rites and Ceremonies', the Mayor of Sunderland, who presided, said: 'Meetings like this are invaluable. Mr. Green has done much to break down barriers between Jews and Christians.' He was recognised in the Jewish community as an expert in this field. At one of the preachers' conferences, Chief Rabbi J. H. Hertz said that inter-faith work required very careful handling. There were very few people who had the fitness to do it, but A. A. Green had put a lifetime into that work and was recognised as a master.

He knew above all what *not* to say, and appreciated the dictum of Philo, the Jewish Alexandrian philosopher, that one should not speak disrespectfully of the religious beliefs of other people. And Green himself remarked that a really British audience would take anything straight from the shoulder if they recognised it was true and if they had faith in the man who was speaking.[4]

Green's concern was not only to interpret Judaism to the Christian world, but also to give young Jews an understanding of the New Testament and of Christianity. In 1921 he announced that he was introducing lessons in the Book of Mark into the syllabus for his senior class at Hampstead. The Jewish community was apprehensive about the scheme, and considerable antagonism was aroused. The 'Jewish Chronicle' attacked it roundly. (The controversy is described in Chapter 7.)

Green was already on bad terms with the 'Chronicle'. In April, 1907, he had commenced a weekly feature in its columns, 'In the Communal Armchair', signed with the pseudonymn 'Tatler'. But his contributions came to an end when the 'Chronicle', which was edited by L. J. Greenberg, a member of Hampstead, criticised him editorially. From that time onwards Green loudly asserted that he never read the 'Chronicle', and when it seemed obvious that he was well acquainted with the paper's contents he would resort to the fiction that 'a friend' had told him what the 'Chronicle' had said on a particular matter.

The centenary history of the 'Jewish Chronicle' describes the unique way in which Green and the paper became reconciled. In 1930 the congregation and some of the communal leaders wished to tender him a public dinner on the occasion of his seventieth birthday. But Mrs. Green was desperately ill, and Green could not face a banquet of that kind knowing that his wife was on her death-bed. If, however, the banquet were postponed, she would guess how serious her illness was.

'What was he to do? Greenberg's sensitive heart was stirred and he hit upon a plan, though he was at this time so crippled by rheumatism (it was just under a year before his own death) that every extra effort was a real agony for him. In connivance with Green, he concocted a bogus report of the banquet. This was set up and a special stereo of one pair of pages for the appropriate week was made. On Thursday, after the paper had been printed, a few copies were run off containing the imaginary report. These were all taken from the machine personally by the editor, who then watched the stereos removed and melted down. One of the fake copies was delivered by him personally to Green's house late that Thursday night. Mrs. Green never suspected anything, and died a few days later. The copy which had brought her so much happiness was returned to the office, and carefully burnt with the others. The banquet never took place.'[5]

In the pulpit Green's tall, imposing stature and powerful dramatic sense made him an impressive figure. As a preacher he took his task very seriously. He was meticulous in his choice of words and his construction of sentences, and the preparation of his sermon was the highlight of his week. Yet he warned his congregation that, important though the literary polish of a sermon was, it was even more important to look for 'the good it conveys, for its truth rather than for its form, for its fervour rather than for its elegance.' His style of preaching was simple, sincere and devotional. His aim was to enter into the personal experiences of his listeners with a word of comfort, of reassurance and of wise guidance, based frequently on the Prophets and the Psalms.

For a time he was lecturer in homiletics at Jews' College. He used to say that the best sermon was not the homiletic or exhortative, but that which had something to teach. Exhortation or analysis of the problems of the community might be very attractive, but would not make the congregation better Jews or better people.

A collection of his sermons was published after his death by a group of his former pupils, and prefaced with an appreciation by Miss Henrietta Adler. This appreciation speaks of him as 'an ideal teacher of religion' with a deep understanding of people – and not only of adults, but of children too. His gifts of imagination 'made the Bible stories live anew and kindled the interest of boys and girls in his classes.'

It is easy to imagine that in all the time he was at Hampstead, no matter how busy he was, he would let nothing interfere with his classes. As long and as often as he possibly could, he took a class himself, as well as acting as honorary superintendent. He even resigned from the post of Chief Officiating Clergyman to the Jewish soldiers in the U.K. in the first World War because it entailed being away from his classes too often. He believed that 'the way to the classroom is also the way to the Synagogue ... Children are bound to the Minister of the congregation in a tie of the utmost value to him and to them as time goes on and the pupils take their places as members of a congregation.'

His own personal efforts were largely responsible for the numbers at the Hampstead classes increasing until they reached a peak of well over 200 and he was able to state, 'So far as my immediate neighbourhood is concerned, I am unaware of even one family where religious instruction of some kind is altogether absent.'[6] Outside his congregation he was vice-president of the Union of Hebrew and Religion Classes which had been founded on the premises of the Hampstead Synagogue in 1908, and a member of the Jewish Memorial Council set up after the first World War 'to make of Judaism a living force throughout the British Empire.'

Green himself, as we have seen, believed that a minister's effectiveness depended on the force of his personality and humanity. Measured against his own standard, Green was one of the most effective of ministers. Despite his eccentricities, he was a man of warm humanity, masterly satire and ready wit. His witticisms are now almost legendary. A famous story relates that the Chief Rabbi on a visit to Hampstead asked whether the men and women in the Synagogue choir sat together. 'Not only do they not sit together,' Green replied, 'but they do not even sing together!'

Someone once suggested that, for the sake of decorum, children should leave the Synagogue before the sermon – to which Green replied by suggesting that everybody should leave. His great fear was that one day on his way to Synagogue he would be run over by a Jewish motor-car; his experience told him that a Jew could drive a motor-car no better on Shabbath than on any other day.

He described a visit which he had paid to the Machzikei Hadath Synagogue, where he had found the congregation *shockling* – swaying in a kind of religious fervour. 'I have never been able to sway a congregation like that!' was his comment. On another occasion he was at a wedding dinner at which the bride's brother proposed a toast to the clergy. Stylishly clad, he languidly remarked in a public-school accent, 'I don't really know why this toast is necessary – after all, we only see our ministers at our Bar Mitzvah receptions and wedding dinners!' At which A. A. Green, looking over the top of his glasses, remarked, 'The young gentleman does us an injustice. Only see us at your Bar Mitzvah receptions and wedding dinners, forsooth! Do we not also visit you in your prisons and in your asylums?'

Green reached the age of 65 in 1925, but was invited to continue in office at Hampstead for a further five years. He retired in 1930, and was presented by the congregation with a testimonial of £3,000. After his retirement he undertook overseas trips to South Africa and America and was warmly welcomed by the Jewish communities in both countries. He died in 1933, and on a memorial tablet in the vestibule of the Synagogue the following was inscribed:

A. A. GREEN

And a book of remembrance was
written before him for them that
feared the Lord and thought upon
his name' (Malachi 3 : 16)

IN MEMORY OF
AARON ASHER GREEN
DEVOTED MINISTER OF
HAMPSTEAD SYNAGOGUE
FROM
ITS FOUNDATION
1892 TILL 1930

CHAPTER V

The Musical Tradition of Hampstead

THE FOUNDERS OF the Synagogue were determined that in the musical quality of the services, as well as in the details of liturgy and ritual, their Synagogue should be distinctive.

Their original idea was to have a purely voluntary choir, but Algernon Lindo, the first choirmaster, felt that there had to be a nucleus of professional voices. Some volunteer choristers were recruited in the early years, and it was due to their assistance that some ambitious choral items could be rendered on special occasions, such as the Hallelujah Chorus from Handel's 'Messiah' which was sung at the reconsecration of the Synagogue after it had been extended in 1901. It gradually became necessary to increase the number of paid choristers until the voluntary element was eventually eliminated, though it was always hoped to compensate for this by a high standard of congregational singing.

In 1896 the choir committee laid down rules and regulations to ensure that every member of the choir co-operated with the choirmaster and showed the right attitude to the service. The rules stated, inter alia: 'Every chorister whilst on duty is actually engaged in the service of God; he must therefore do his best to render the singing as efficient as possible, and also by orderly conduct to make himself worthy of the position which he holds.'

There was a chorister's prayer taken from the liturgy: 'May the words of our mouths and the meditations of our hearts be acceptable before thee, O Lord.' The choristers were paid a salary varying from under £15 to £30 a year, and they could be fined for a breach of the rules or for being absent from the service or from a rehearsal.

In the contentious atmosphere in which the choir commenced as a mixed choir (though Hampstead was not the first constituent of the United Synagogue to introduce female choristers), its development became a matter of critical interest to the congregation and, while the old set of strict rules and fines is no longer insisted upon, the choir committee has always been one of the most active committees of the board of management. Its chairman for very many years was Henry Gledhill, who served both Hampstead and the United Synagogue in many important offices.

The first choirmaster, Algernon Lindo, resigned in 1896 on being appointed choirmaster at the Bayswater Synagogue. He was succeeded by Louis Freeman, previously a member of the choir, who held office for nearly twenty years, until his death in 1915. The Rev. S. Manné, the first chazan, who is said to have had 'a voice to bewitch,' resigned from Hampstead in April, 1899, and the congregation assisted him with his passage to Johannesburg.

While the search for a permanent chazan was proceeding, the Rev. Wolf Stoloff was engaged as temporary reader. A large number of chazanim applied for the vacant position. Applications came from all over the United Kingdom, as well as from the U.S.A. and several continental countries, but it was Stoloff who, in 1902, was given the permanent appointment. For some years he also, rather unwillingly, had to act as secretary. For many years he served the congregation faithfully and conscientiously. He was relieved of the burden of the secretaryship in 1910, when B. M. Woolf was appointed to the position.

Stoloff was not the most melodious of cantors, but he had a fine musical knowledge. He was a model exponent of the traditional reading of the Scriptures and published a book on the subject, as well as an edition of the Friday evening service with musical notations.[1] One of his particular interests was the children of the congregation, for whom he conducted a special *Haphtarah* class. Between Stoloff and A. A. Green relations were not always cordial. They were two totally different personalities, hailing from contrasting backgrounds – Green from an anglicised background and Stoloff from a so-called 'foreign' one – and there were times when Green's quick wit was employed at the expense of his colleague. For a few years before Stoloff's retirement in 1931 the Synagogue had the services of an assistant reader, the Rev. H. Cooper, who was able to enhance the musical side of congregational worship. Stoloff died in 1952.

The Rev. Gershon Boyars, then with the Birmingham Hebrew Congregation, was appointed chazan in 1931. Boyars had a genius for friendship, and he quickly gained the affection of the congregation. Born in Russia, he had spent his youth in Liverpool and had studied music in America. In the first World War he saw service in the Middle East. He had been chazan of the Western Synagogue before going to Birmingham. He was a Hebrew scholar and a chazan with a rare power of insight into the prayers he recited, and between him and Samuel Alman, his choirmaster, there developed a musical partnership in which the one inspired the other.

Until Alman came to Hampstead in 1916, the service had been dominated by the melodies of Mombach, in whose choir A. A. Green had sung as a youth. Some use was made of the compositions of Sulzer, Naumbourg and Lewandowski, and the English chazan-composers, Hast and Wasserzug. But in the last half-century there has hardly been a choral service at Hampstead in which Alman's own compositions have not been represented. He attempted to combine Jewish content with modern harmony, stressing the correct accentuation and pronunciation of the Hebrew words. Many of his settings were specially composed for use at Hampstead, and the congregation helped him to publish his two volumes of compositions.

It was a matter for deep regret to Hampstead that a proposal made in 1947 that Alman should have a special position created for him by the United Synagogue – 'of such a nature that he should be able to devote his great talent to composing further music which will be of great value to this and also to future generations' – had not been realised before Alman's death a few months later. Alman's partnership with Boyars was described in these words by the Rev. Dr. Isaac Levy:

> 'There was indeed a wonderful association between chazan and composer. The one poured forth his compositions as the spirit moved him, the other giving loving expression to the melodies which he knew were so often written specially for him. The inspiration which both enjoyed was frequently mutually created and it is thanks to their close friendship that synagogal liturgical music has been so enriched.'

In 1959 Boyars retired after 28 years as chazan, and on 4th July conducted his final service. On a crescendo of musical perfection and human emotion a long and historic chapter came to an end. In honour of the occasion Henry Gledhill, who had been warden when Boyars was appointed to Hampstead, and who had subsequently held high office in the United Synagogue, sat in the wardens' box and joined in the tributes paid at a farewell reception a few days later. Boyars himself once wrote: 'No one will accuse me of exaggeration if I claim that we, at Hampstead, have the finest repertoire of any Synagogue in London or, for that matter, of any of the provincial Synagogues in this country.' It was a claim founded on fact, and that fact itself was largely of Boyars' own making. Boyars died in 1963, aged 68.

The Rev. Charles Lowy was inducted into office as his successor on 11th July, 1959. Born in Pressburg, Bratislava, into a family of chazanim, Mr. Lowy's Jewish education was gained at the *yeshivoth* of Galanta, Tselem and Pressburg.

He studied music in Vienna, Budapest and at the State Conservatoire in Munich. Before coming to Britain he was Oberkantor at the Reichenbach Synagogue in Munich and the Rombach Synagogue in Budapest. He gave recitals of liturgical music on Radio Budapest, and also officiated at the famous Tabak-Tempel in that city. For eleven years he was First Reader at the Queen's Park Synagogue in Glasgow, and now worthily maintains the distinctive quality of Hampstead's services. Like his predecessor he combines scholarship, personality, deep understanding of traditional Synagogue music and a high standard of musicianship. Some of his own compositions now enhance the Synagogue's musical repertoire.

Since the death of Samuel Alman the choirmasters at Hampstead have been Bernard Cousin, Dudley Cohen and Willy Scharf.

CHAPTER VI

Social Service

1892 WAS THE year in which Claude Montefiore's Hibbert lectures appeared, an event that symbolised the religious restlessness among the older, middle-class community. The same year saw the publication of Israel Zangwill's 'Children of the Ghetto', which portrayed for the first time the vast immigrant community that had grown up so rapidly in the East End in the previous decade.

The native and the newcomer represented almost two worlds. Despite his dignity and diplomacy, Hermann Adler and the West End Jews who idolised him were regarded as suspect by the newcomers, and though the West made strenuous efforts to improve conditions in the East, there was a strong element of patronising philanthropy characterising their efforts. This is, however, not to minimise the value of these philanthropic endeavours in which Hampstead was a pioneer, and which gave way within a generation to a greater sense of understanding and unity between the two sections of the community.

Since the founders of the Hampstead Synagogue were mostly long-settled and well-to-do, they were in a position to work actively for a variety of social service projects. In October, 1892, the women of the congregation formed a ladies' guild under the leadership of Mrs. Frank I. Lyons, Mrs. Herbert Bentwich, Mrs. John Meredith and Mrs. A. A. Green. The objects of the guild were to make and collect garments for the poor, to promote welfare work in the Hampstead district itself, and to carry out visitation in East London.

The hope of the Hampstead congregation was that each

61

London Synagogue would take on the responsibility for a defined area of East London, and although this ideal was not completely realised, A. A. Green chose the area around Old Montague Street, E.1. for the particular attention of Hampstead members, and he commenced visitation with the assistance of the guild. A direct outcome of this work was the establishment of the Butler Street Girls' Club, which opened in two rooms in Old Montague Street made available by Abraham Davis, who subsequently served as an honorary officer of Hampstead. As the first annual report of the Synagogue put it, rather quaintly :

'The Hampstead Synagogue Guild has continued during the past year its missionary work in East London. It is impossible to over-estimate the value of the services of these ladies . . . They have succeeded in carrying some little light to illumine the clouded lives of some of our un-fortunate co-religionists, and they have the satisfaction of knowing that the work of the Hampstead Synagogue Guild is a recognised force for good in East London, and an often quoted model of earnestness and thoroughness.'

The report continued by stating that weekly meetings were held in the Old Montague Street premises, at which 'a bright evening is passed, to which the humble guests of the Hampstead Synagogue look forward with constant pleasure.' At the same time, the work of the Board of Guardians (now the Jewish Welfare Board), which was then situated in Middlesex Street, E.1, was supported by the establishment of a canvassing committee in Hampstead, which continued to raise considerable sums for the Board for many years.

A. A. Green himself was untiring in his efforts in the East End. Apart from widespread welfare work, he acted as Jewish chaplain or as United Synagogue representative to a number of institutions and committees. He had known the East End from his youth and had, years before, conducted the first branch of the Jewish Religious Education Board in

Settles Street. Now he frequently inspected Hebrew classes in various parts of the East End and, by February, 1893, when he had been in Hampstead barely six months, he had to decline a further invitation of this kind, writing to Herbert Bentwich :

'I have been seriously thinking this matter over and it appears to me that in extra-synagogal work we are doing in the East as much as we can undertake well. No other Synagogue does what we do and, as our East End work promises developments which will tax all our resources, I .am inclined to decline for the present this suggested addition.'

Hampstead members were prominent in the Jewish Lads' Brigade, founded in 1895 'to train its members in loyalty, honour, discipline and self-respect, that they shall become worthy and useful citizens, and a credit to their country and their community.' They also worked in the youth club movement, which was consolidated as the Jewish Athletic Association in 1899 and became the Association for Jewish Youth in 1927. A further East End charity which Hampstead supported was the Children's Country Holiday Fund.

The favourite Hampstead cause for very many years has been the Norwood Home for Jewish Children. A. A. Green and Frank I. Lyons established a Hampstead Orphan Aid Society in 1893, and the children of the Hampstead classes brought a penny each for Norwood when they came to classes every Sunday. The Society intensified its activities from about 1925, when an adult section was formed, and since 1933 the main annual function has been a dinner and ball. For a long period the president and guiding light of the Society was Michael Cohen.

In addition to their collections for Norwood, the children of the Hampstead classes also brought toys and games to the children's Chanukah service for distribution among children in the East End.

In the early years of this century, when pogroms in Russia aroused a world-wide reaction, one of the honorary officers of Hampstead, Carl Stettauer, took the lead in investigating the situation of Russian Jewry and allocating relief funds. In 1905 Stettauer went to Russia at some personal risk, and achieved world-wide acclaim for his work. He was later treasurer of the United Synagogue. He maintained a close association with Hampstead until his death in 1913.

Ladies' Guild

A number of other examples of welfare work initiated at Hampstead could be mentioned. At one stage the ladies' guild was concerned with the training of Jewish girls for domestic service and, led by Mrs. Caroline Nathan, established a domestic training home in West Hampstead which later moved to Adelaide Road and finally to Highbury Grove. In the first World War the congregation opened two hostels in Greencroft Gardens and Compayne Gardens for Belgian refugees 'of education and refinement and of previous prosperity', and 25 children from these hostels joined the Synagogue classes. By 1917, when most of the refugees had found work, the hostels were closed.

In the second World War the ladies' guild worked energetically for Jewish refugees and for families who had been made homeless in the air raids. For many years the guild, under the leadership of Mrs. Sara Simpson, was also responsible for sending thousands of beautifully made garments to charitable institutions. Thanks to Mrs. Isaac Levy and her desire for wider community activity, the guild also launched a programme of social and cultural activities, which make it today a vital element in congregational life. In the new community centre there is a special Guild Room dedicated to the memory of Mrs. Simpson.

Flourishing organisations like the Friendship Club movement and the Jewish Deaf Association received their first great impetus at Hampstead, and there can hardly be a worthy cause that does not attract generous support from the members of the congregation.

Zionism

Zionist work does not go back very far in Hampstead, though in the 1890's some congregational personalities like Herbert Bentwich and Leopold J. Greenberg were ardent supporters of Herzl. In fact, it was not far from the Hampstead Synagogue that Herzl visited Israel Zangwill in 1895 in an attempt to arouse support for the idea of a Jewish state. Zangwill was living in Kilburn at the time and the Zionist historian, Josef Fraenkel, has written that 'modern Zionism in London began when Herzl entered Zangwill's study'.

The English Zionist Federation was formed in 1899, with Herbert Bentwich as its first chairman, despite Hermann Adler's attacks on the movement as 'an egregious blunder' and the opposition of other notable figures, such as Israel Abrahams, Claude Montefiore and Lucien Wolf. The 'Jewish Chronicle' was also critical of Zionism until Leopold J. Greenberg became editor in 1907. Congregations like Hampstead showed little sympathy towards the movement at this period, which may partly account for the disillusionment which led Herbert Bentwich to leave the Synagogue. Bentwich henceforth worshipped when in London at the Spanish and Portuguese Synagogue, Lauderdale Road, where his friend and fellow-Zionist, Haham Dr. Gaster, preached.

It is not generally known that A. A. Green regarded himself as 'an ardent Zionist, anxious to see Palestine once more in possession of our people, its classic ground tenanted once again by the heirs of its former possessors, its fields and vineyards smiling with fertility in response to the labour of Jewish hands, its cities and its villages once more the home of an Israel which, with the help of Jewish courage and perseverance, shall be a nation once again.' Green wrote these words in an article in 'Young Jewry' in January, 1898, but had to admit that 'many of our best and wisest share neither my expectation nor even my hope, and regard Zionism as an impossibility.'

A change in attitude became evident after the issue of the Balfour Declaration in 1917, and by 1928 the annual meeting at Hampstead could carry unanimously a resolution moved by George Tibber and Harry Samuels, expressing satisfaction at 'extension of the support for the work for the upbuilding of Palestine.'

Since the second World War Hampstead has become one of the most Israel-minded of congregations. Efforts for Israeli causes meet with a large-scale response; the Hampstead committee of the Joint Palestine Appeal, for instance, headed by J. C. Gilbert, collects a considerable sum each year. The attempts to introduce the Israeli pronunciation of Hebrew into the service also indicate a desire for a strong association between Hampstead and the Jewish state.

Votes for Women

The amendment of the United Synagogue Act in February, 1954, which granted the franchise to women who were members of Synagogues in their own right, was another cause in which Hampstead displayed a pioneer spirit. The congregation repeatedly confirmed its desire to give women the opportunity to play an active part in Synagogue life and a voice in the shaping of congregational policy.

As early as 1913, Dr. Jacob Snowman submitted a resolution to the annual meeting of the Synagogue that lady seat-holders be granted the right to vote at Synagogue elections. Emil Kahn, the chairman, said that having taken the opinions of the honorary solicitor and the secretary of the United Synagogue, he had come to the conclusion that the motion was out of order and could not be considered. Dr. Snowman re-introduced his motion in modified terms the next year, and this time it was passed by 13 votes to 10.

On 29th May, 1919, the Council of the United Synagogue set up a special committee to examine the United Synagogue

Act. The terms of reference were general, and there was no specific mention of votes for women seat-holders. By early 1923, no report had emerged and at the Synagogue annual meeting, Herbert Michaelis moved an instruction to the Hampstead representatives on the Council 'to do their utmost to *expedite* the passage of an amendment to the United Synagogue Act, conferring voting power on lady seat-holders.' The meeting carried the motion, and Samuel Moses stated that the special committee were unanimously in favour of giving women the vote. In fact, they recommended accordingly at a Council meeting in November.

Most of the constituent Synagogues favoured the measure, but it was rejected when it came before a special meeting in 1926. But its advocates were not so easily defeated. At the next annual meeting at Hampstead, held in May, 1927, Herbert Michaelis secured unanimous support for the following resolution:

'That, in view of the pronouncement of the Chief Rabbi that there is no objection whatsoever in Jewish Law to the grant of voting rights to Women Seat-holders, this meeting declares itself in favour of this measure and pledges itself to support any action which may be taken to attain that end.'

A new effort was made in 1928 to amend the United Synagogue Act, but again to no avail. Pending the attainment of their declared aim, Hampstead decided that women seat-holders would at least be permitted to attend general meetings of the congregation and to take part in the discussions, and to be represented on congregational sub-committees. In fact, ladies had been serving on the classes committee for some years before this.

In 1931 Herbert Michaelis asked the annual meeting to instruct the congregation's representatives to urge that the whole matter be re-opened, and as usual by now his resolution was carried unanimously, as it was on the next occasion he raised the subject, which was in 1943. In 1946 and 1947 others (particularly Mrs. S. R. Lissack) took up the cudgels. Again Hampstead unanimously declared itself in favour of voting rights for women, and within the congregation itself it was now arranged that representatives of the ladies' guild would be invited to board meetings. The board decided to press the matter actively and to canvass support among the other Synagogues, but they found only one other congregation prepared to back Hampstead, and in the circumstances felt that the only thing to do was to leave the matter alone for the time being.

In 1949, J. C. Gilbert, then a warden, put a resolution before the congregation urging strongly 'the immediate and serious consideration' of the question by the United Synagogue Council, and again in 1950 a similar expression of the congregation's views was made. This time J. C. Gilbert was able to say that, though previous resolutions from Hampstead had not received much support from other Synagogues, there now seemed to be a chance of something being achieved. However, in 1951, the position still remained much the same as it had been for so long, and Mark Kleiner, now the warden president, moved the now traditional resolution on the subject.

Eventually, three years later, a meeting of representatives from all Synagogues was convened to consider alterations to the United Synagogue Act. On the question of votes for women, guidance was sought from the Chief Rabbi, Dr. Brodie. Like his predecessor, he gave the principle his blessing, stating: 'I rule that women who are members of the United Synagogue in their own right may vote at all meetings. Such women members are, however, not to be voted for.'

At last some action was taken. The wheels of progress had moved slowly, but they had moved. At the annual meeting at Hampstead in 1954, the warden president, Michael Abrahams, was able to say that among the interesting events of the past year had been the acceptance of the proposal for women's voting rights, of which Herbert Michaelis had been a leading protagonist for over a quarter of a century. The United Synagogue Act had been changed, and Mr. Abrahams congratulated Mrs. Mary Wollman on being the first woman in the Hampstead congregation to register her vote.

CHAPTER VII

Jewish Education

ONE OF THE first signs of Jewish life in the district was the commencement of Hebrew and religion classes on 31st May, 1891, under the auspices of a committee of which Herbert Bentwich was chairman.

Israel Abrahams, then a lecturer at Jews' College, and the Rev. Isidore Myers, an Australian-born scholar who later became a minister in San Francisco, were both invited to conduct the Hampstead classes. When both replied that they were not available, the committee appointed Dr. Wolf Heinemann, who had formerly been on the staff of University College School and was then lecturing in Hebrew at the Polytechnic, at a salary of ten shillings a week. Dr. Heinemann later went to Dunedin, New Zealand, and became a prominent figure in education and Jewish affairs there.

The classes opened under Dr. Heinemann at the West Hampstead Town Hall and met on Sundays from 11–12 for Hebrew and from 12–1 for Bible history and religion. No fees were charged, but children were expected to bring a prayer-book and Bible. Subsequently the classes moved to Lauriston Lodge, which then stood on the site of the proposed Synagogue. In September, 1892 A. A. Green took over the superintendence of the classes, informing the members of the congregation :

'I feel it is hardly necessary to point out the great value of classes of this character. It will be our aim to make them a potent influence for good in the education of the young, rendering them the means for the deepening of the religious sentiment, for the awakening of interest in Hebrew literature and for the increase of information concerning the past of Judaism and its potentialities for the future ... I earnestly trust that we may be favoured with your hearty co-operation. There cannot possibly emanate from the Synagogue a higher claim.'

The text-books adopted for the classes were, for the first class, the Bible, the newly issued Authorised Daily Prayer Book edited by the Rev. Simeon Singer, and the 'Text-Book of the Jewish Religion' by Dr. M. Friedländer, principal of Jews' College. The second and third classes used Abrahams' 'Standard Prayer Book' and Friedländer's 'Religion'.

The syllabus was geared to the Chief Rabbi's Code, introduced by Nathan Marcus Adler, which divided Hebrew, Bible, and Jewish history and religion into eight standards for infants and elementary classes. It was admitted to be a minimal syllabus for classes which, like those at Hampstead, met for a very short time on Sundays, and bore no real relation to the intensive study that was carried on in the *cheder* and *Talmud Torah* classes in the East End at the time.

A. A. Green conducted an advanced class which met on the Sabbath during some years and at other times on various week-day evenings. It aimed to introduce young men and women to the classic works of Jewish literature, usually in translation, and over the years the Psalms, the Ethics of the Fathers, and the Books of Kings, Isaiah, Jeremiah and Job were among those studied. At different periods the classes also included a singing period conducted by the Synagogue choirmaster, and a *Haphtarah* class conducted by the chazan.

An annual examination of the classes was held with a prominent outside personality acting as inspector, and minutes of the classes' committee meetings are full of conscientious discussion of the detailed reports which the examiners submitted. Frequently the reports praised the efficient methods adopted in the classes and it is noteworthy

71

that, as early as 1902, the examiner for that year, Dayan Asher Feldman, mentioned that the children in the top class were learning colloquial Hebrew phrases and suggested that this should be introduced throughout the school.

The number of children attending the classes was 72 in 1892 and continued to grow. In order to accommodate them a set of classrooms was erected at the side of the Synagogue, Frank I. Lyons laying the foundation stone in June, 1897. The welfare of Hebrew education was a matter of deep concern to Lyons, and he worked for the classes with phenomenal energy.

He persistently advocated the co-ordination of Synagogue religion classes throughout London, and at a conference held at Hampstead in 1908, the Union of Hebrew and Religion Classes was formed under his presidency. Lyons later also became president of the Jewish Religious Education Board. (After the second World War these organisations merged with the Talmud Torah Trust to become the London Board of Jewish Religious Education.) When the Central Committee for Jewish Education was set up by the Jewish Memorial Council, Lyons became vice-president.

The enrolment at Hampstead increased steadily. At the time the Union was established there were nearly 200 pupils, and some classes had to meet in the Synagogue itself, separated by screens. In addition to those who came to the Synagogue classes, a large number received private tuition (many from either Green or Stoloff). A picture of the position, albeit incomplete, emerges from the replies to a circular which A. A. Green sent out to members of the congregation in 1910.

Of the 97 replies which were received (representing a small percentage of the total membership) 19 members said they had no children of school age; and of those who did have children, 50 children were attending the religion classes, 84 were receiving private instruction, and 9 were both attending the classes and receiving private instruction. In addition,

Mount Zion – stained glass window designed by B. Sochachewsky

Dayan Mark Gollop, B.A.

a number of children were at boarding schools, and 20 girls attending South Hampstead High School formed a class held there by A. A. Green.

War conditions affected the enrolment, and by 1919 it had dropped as low as 43. In 1921 Lyons laid the foundation stone of further additional classrooms (on the site of Dr. Jacob Snowman's stable in Kingdon Road), and the roll quickly climbed back up to 183. By the mid-1920's it reached its peak of well over 200.

The outbreak of the second World War, with the consequent evacuation of children from London, had an adverse effect on the classes, and for two periods during the war they had to close down completely. Since then, however, the average enrolment has been about 125, and today it is over 160. There is still a sizeable minority of Hampstead children at boarding schools, and a number have private tuition, though their proportion is much lower than when the 1910 survey was carried out.

The two great changes in the educational picture in recent years have concerned the classrooms and the syllabus. The new community centre contains five up-to-date and well-equipped classrooms, so that the conditions under which teachers and children work are better than ever before. However, the addition of these rooms has not obviated the necessity to use the older classrooms too, and there is still a mild accommodation problem.

While the standard of attainment at Hampstead in the past was similar to that at many other Synagogue classes, the aim of the London Board of Jewish Religious Education since the war has been to raise standards considerably, and a comparison of the present-day Hampstead syllabus with those of the 1890's indicates that this has been achieved to some extent. The classes meet today on Sunday mornings (for three hours) and on Monday and Wednesday evenings (for $1\frac{1}{2}$ hours each time), though the weekday attendance is much lower than that on Sundays.

The elementary classes aim to teach children to read and write in Hebrew, to conduct a simple Hebrew conversation, to become acquainted with the main features of the prayer-book, to translate simple passages from the Pentateuch and to acquire a basic knowledge of Jewish history and religion. Older pupils can take courses leading to the annual examinations of the London Board and to the General Certificate of Education in Classical Hebrew, Modern Hebrew and Religious Knowledge.

There is also a special class for girls in which they are prepared for the Bat Mitzvah test and ceremony. All instruction is given in the Israeli pronunciation of Hebrew. Children's services take place every Sabbath and Festival morning, and there is an active parents' association, which works to provide amenities for the children and to arouse interest in the classes.

West Hampstead Day School

For a short period a Jewish day school, the first in north-west London, operated in the classrooms of the Hampstead Synagogue. This was the West Hampstead Jewish Day School, founded in 1927 by two leading members of the congregation, Emanuel Snowman and Harry Samuels, with the sanction of the board of management of the Synagogue. For some years another distinguished member, Hugh Harris (now literary editor of the 'Jewish Chronicle'), was head-master. The school soon outgrew the accommodation available at Hampstead and eventually moved into premises in Willesden. Owing to evacuation the school closed in the second World War, but it was the forerunner of the various Jewish day schools now flourishing in north-west London.

New Testament Instruction

The annual report of the Synagogue classes in 1921 stated: 'Several members of the Advanced Class have expressed a

74

desire to have a course which will include some guidance in the understanding of the position of the New Testament. The Superintendent is still considering the point, but it indicates the live interest of the members of the Class in the understanding of their theological position.'

The 'Jewish World' of 3rd November reported that A. A. Green had in fact commenced to expound the book of Mark, claiming to have obtained the Chief Rabbi's approval for his action. The paper said it was difficult to believe that Green could find this consistent with his position as a Jewish minister (or indeed as a Jew), and almost impossible to believe that the Chief Rabbi would have given any sort of consent. It called upon the Chief Rabbi to issue a strong repudiation.

Two weeks went by, and the paper returned to the attack, demanding: 'Now, then, Dr. Hertz, tell us. Do you or don't you? It is a simple question, and can best be answered with a still simpler "Yes" or "No".' Rabbi Dr. Isaac Herzog of Dublin (later Chief Rabbi of Israel) wrote to the 'Jewish Chronicle' expressing consternation that there had been no disclaimer from the Chief Rabbi.

On 21st November Dr. Hertz issued a statement which said:

'Some time ago I learned from the Rev. A. A. Green of the repeated request to him by some of his elder pupils to be instructed as to the Jewish attitude towards the New Testament. I have always felt that for any Jewish teacher or parent to refuse definite guidance on a subject so vital to Jewish young men and women would be absolutely indefensible. I accordingly advised him to arrange a course, say, of three informal talks by men who had a mastery of the subject: and I mentioned the names of men of unswerving orthodoxy whose help would be of the utmost value in this direction. The Rev. A. A. Green had, however, in the meantime discussed the question with one of these very men, and this gentleman represented to him

75

that the best way of grappling with this delicate problem was to go straight to the sources, read selected portions of the New Testament, and explain these in the light of Jewish tradition and belief. While I still hold that a few informal talks would have been sufficient, I did not feel justified in disallowing the suggestion made by an eminent scholar.'

Both the 'Jewish World' and the 'Jewish Chronicle' now opened their columns to lengthy correspondence on the subject. Some letters supported Green. S. T. Cohn, chairman of the classes committee of the Hampstead Synagogue, wrote claiming that the matter had been misrepresented and that there was no question of introducing New Testament instruction into the ordinary classes but only into the advanced class. This he wrote, consisted of 'pupils of adult age' (their average age was subsequently given as 20 by Samuel Moses), some of whom were University graduates.

Most correspondents, however, supported the critical stand taken by the two papers and asked how the Chief Rabbi could reconcile his attitude with Jewish tradition, notwithstanding the advice of the unnamed 'eminent scholar' (who was Adolph Büchler, the principal of Jews' College).

Green devoted his sermon on 26th November to a defence of his point of view. He said the members of his class had asked for an explanation of New Testament teaching because they were constantly mingling with Christian friends and needed to know what Judaism had to say about the claims of Christianity. In addition, he was concerned that some young Jews of whose cases he was aware had come under the influence of conversionist propaganda, and he wanted to be able to prevent these young people being won over.

The matter was raised at a meeting of the United Synagogue Council on 28th November, and it was decided that, 'the question of the use of part of the premises of the

76

Hampstead Synagogue for the purpose of imparting instruction in the New Testament be referred to the Ecclesiastical
Authorities for their opinion and report to the Council.'

Samuel Moses of Hampstead argued, however, that the
real point at issue was not the purpose to which Synagogue
premises could be put, but that young Jewish adults had a
right to learn something about religions other than their
own. Dr. Jacob Snowman said that in his view Green was
doing 'an excellent piece of work', even though the method
that had been adopted might not have been the most
desirable. Some speakers thought the motion was tantamount
to a vote of no confidence in the Chief Rabbi, but most felt
that it was essential to discuss a matter which had caused
such a stir in the community.

The press controversy continued for many weeks. A
number of Rabbis and laymen argued strongly that for an
orthodox minister to teach the New Testament in Synagogue
classes was completely against Jewish law and sentiment.
Among those who expressed this view were Rabbis Isaac
Herzog (Dublin), I. J. Yoffey (Manchester), Y. M. Sandelson
(Newcastle) and Isidore Epstein (Middlesbrough, later
principal of Jews' College). The last-named said that
Green's action was 'as grave and serious an offence as
that of King Manasseh in setting up an idol in the Holy
Temple.'

Protest meetings were held in several cities. 'Mentor' of
the 'Jewish Chronicle' (Leopold J. Greenberg) wrote of a
visit to some of the provincial towns: 'In the whole course
of my experience I have never known any question that
aroused so much real passion and indignation.' He added
that more criticism was being directed against the Chief Rabbi
than against A. A. Green, because it should have been the
duty of the Chief Rabbi to tell Green plainly that he could
not allow something which violated Jewish tradition.

By the end of December the weight of public opinion had
become so strong that, even though the Beth Din had not

77

yet issued a ruling, only one course remained open to Green and the Hampstead Synagogue, and that course they took. They announced that the New Testament teaching was to be abandoned. The 'Jewish Chronicle' welcomed the decision. 'Mr. Green has gravely erred,' the paper wrote, 'but that must not in the least blind the community to the considerable services he has performed for Judaism throughout his career, to the excellence of his ministration and to his zeal in championing the Jewish cause.' 'Mentor', in a further comment, remarked that the community had not heard the whole story of the controversy, which was really a 'pretty intrigue' in which Green had been used by others whose identities 'Mentor' only hinted at.

In view of the attitude Green took on this occasion, it is interesting to consider his part in a controversy in 1929, when the Committee of Ministers issued a new prayer-book for children's services on Rosh Hashanah and Yom Kippur. The book contained (p. 128) Isaac Watts' hymn, 'O God our help in ages past', which is a poetic paraphrase of the 90th Psalm, and also (p. 7) a metrical version of Psalm 148, 'Praise the Lord, ye heavens adore Him', set to music by Haydn.

Green objected strongly to the inclusion of non-Jewish hymns, and his views were given publicity in the 'Jewish Chronicle'. The Chief Rabbi, Dr. Hertz, accused Green of having, through his strictures in the Press, committed 'an act of disloyalty to the Chief Rabbi and to Mr. Green's colleagues who were responsible for the publication.' Dr. Hertz added that he saw no reason to veto the inclusion in the book of the versions of the Psalms referred to, which were only English Psalms, and he 'could not declare their inclusion in the Book as something heretical.' At a meeting of the Committee of Ministers a resolution of support for the Chief Rabbi's attitude was passed unanimously, those present comprising, among others, two Dayanim of the London Beth Din.

Courses for girls

In 1889, three years before the Synagogue was opened, the committee recommended:

'That a service for the confirmation of girls, to follow examination and to be held at times to be determined hereafter, be instituted in the proposed Synagogue, following the model of the service adopted at the Central Synagogue.'

Both Nathan Marcus Adler and Hermann Adler agreed to the proposal. Consecration services for girls had been instituted in the Bayswater Synagogue in 1864, and the conditions under which the Chief Rabbi had permitted them there and, from 1889 onwards, in the Central Synagogue, included the avoidance of the term 'confirmation' with its Christian overtones and the holding of the ceremony on a weekday and not on a Sabbath.

The Hampstead congregation now accepted these conditions, abandoning the name 'confirmation' and referring instead to 'special services for girls', of which the first was held under A. A. Green's superintendence in July, 1895. From time to time similar services took place, and from about 1924 the Chief Rabbi, Dr. Hertz, actively advocated the idea, drawing up a syllabus and an order of service for the occasion. In 1925 Dr. Hertz declared:

'I have sanctioned the special consecration service for girls mainly because of the prescribed course of instruction in the knowledge of Judaism preparatory to such consecration service – a course of study that acquaints them with the teaching and story of Israel, and equips them for life's duties with an understanding of the principles and practices of our holy faith. Those ministers who have completed this course with the girls under their charge speak with enthusiasm of the new outlook which such study and serious preparation give both to the girls and their parents.'[1]

Dayan Gollop, in a sermon on Shavuoth, 1931 and shortly afterwards in a letter to the Hampstead congregation, stated that he intended to re-institute the practice in Hampstead, explaining: 'The consecration of girls is intended to be the equivalent of the Bar Mitzvah ceremony for boys and I should like to see parents, as well as children, looking forward to that ceremony with the same pleasurable anticipation as for the boys' Bar Mitzvah.'

Only one consecration service was held at Hampstead in the immediate post-war years because of difficulties in obtaining official sanction for the scheme, but in 1965 a special course for girls aged 12 and over was commenced, culminating in a ceremony held on a Sunday morning in July, 1966, which followed the general lines of the order of service issued by Dr. Hertz in 1924. The syllabus as formulated for the 1965 class covered the practical duties of the Jewish woman, the place of women in Jewish life, an outline of Jewish history and religious practice, and the study of famous Jewish women through the ages. It is intended to make this an annual ceremony.

G.C.E. Classes

Another innovation in 1965 was the establishment of a senior department of the classes, gearing its work to the General Certificate of Education at Ordinary Level. Classes were arranged in Classical Hebrew, Modern Hebrew and Religious Knowledge, and the initial enrolment in the department was 25 pupils, whose average age was 14.

Youth Activities

Children's services have been held more or less regularly ever since 1892, both on Sabbaths and on Holydays. In 1925 Hampstead introduced in addition the idea of special provision for young adults of the congregation. Under ideal conditions, it was admitted, the place for children and adolescents was in the Synagogue itself at the side of their parents. However, it was just when the Synagogue was at its fullest, on the High Holydays, that this ideal became a practical impossibility, and the young people were crowded out. It was therefore decided in the first place to arrange for services for adolescents on Rosh Hashanah and Yom Kippur.

The experiment amply justified itself. These were not the usual children's services; they were deliberately arranged so as to follow the lines of the ordinary adult service, and one of the earliest projects undertaken by Dayan Gollop was the erection of a special Junior Synagogue, which was opened by Mr. John Lewis in July, 1935 (and which is used during the week as a *beth hamidrash* for morning and evening services) and the publication of a prayer-book for use at these services.

A further development from these facilities was a Junior Membership scheme, worked out by Lionel Herman, in which sons of members or non-members of the congregation aged between 13 and 21 were enrolled as junior members, with their own junior board and president, with the aim of giving them experience in communal work and synagogue administration. The first junior board consisted of Philip B. Levy, Stanley Charig, Harold Gollop, Ronald Kaufman and S. C. S. de Wolfe, all of whom subsequently became leading figures in communal life. In addition, the Hampstead Young People's Association was formed to provide social and cultural activities for the over-16 age group.

With the coming of the second World War, attempts were made to maintain youth activities, but without great success. After the war a succession of youth clubs has been organised, some achieving a fair degree of success, but for many years inadequate premises limited activities. Today, when the congregation possesses its fine community centre, the youth committee is energetically working to provide a variety of groups ranging from Cubs and Brownies to a young adults' social club, and catering for every age group and interest.

The youth services instituted in 1925 are still maintained, though on a somewhat different basis. On the High Holydays there are, in addition to services for young children, a youth service for the 11–14 age group, and a young adults' service for those aged 15 and over. In recent years it has been customary on Simchath Torah morning to put the emphasis on the youth of the congregation, with all the *mitzvoth* going to the boys, and the reading of the Torah and *Haphtarah* being undertaken by them.[2]

From time to time youth services are held in the main Synagogue itself, with boys and young men conducting most of the service, and the sermon being devoted to them. There was once a feeling that Hampstead was an elderly congregation with very few young people, but if this was ever true, today it is a thing of the past, and there is no lack of children and young people associated with the congregation.

Adult Education

Notable among communal institutions at the turn of the century was the literary society movement, which served Jewish adult education by means of 'the diffusion of a knowledge of Jewish literature, history and sociology.' Dr. Jacob Snowman, a vice-president of the Union of Jewish Literary Societies, convened a private meeting in September, 1902, to set up a society in north-west London, and as a result the Hampstead and St. John's Wood Jewish Literary Society came into existence with an initial membership of 150.

Its first honorary officers were: Samuel Moses, president; the Revs. A. A. Green and H. L. Price, vice-presidents; B. M. Benjamin, treasurer; and Horace L. Friedlander and D. Manchevsky, honorary secretaries. The subjects of lectures and debates in the early years ranged over a wide field of politics, religion, art, science and literature, faithfully reflecting the interests and issues of the time, and in addition concerts, conversaziones and balls were held. The society continued in existence for a long period, in more recent years with Miss Miriam Joseph as honorary secretary, maintaining a varied programme of cultural and social activities.

There did, however, remain a gap in congregational educational work, despite the efforts of the literary society. The need for more intensive courses in Jewish subjects for adults was partly met by A. A. Green's advanced class, and in 1928 a sub-committee was set up 'to explore the subject of Jewish adult education, and to report to the board of management'. The outcome was the arrangement of several courses of lectures on Jewish history, Jewish literature and the Talmud, with the co-operation of neighbouring Synagogues. Before long, Hampstead was left to bear the whole responsibility, and a spirit of pessimism developed as attendances became meagre. When Dayan Gollop came to Hampstead he threw himself energetically into the movement and arranged a number of Sunday morning talks, evening study circles and the like. Among the notable meetings he organised were a celebration of the 800th anniversary of Mainonides' birth, a lecture by the Chief Rabbi on the Hebrew University of Jerusalem, and an address by the renowned historian, G. P. Gooch.

In the post-war years the ministers of the congregation have likewise actively fostered adult education. Several courses of lectures took place at Hampstead under the University of London extension committee in association with Jews' College, and for many years the Rev. Dr. Isaac Levy drew large attendances at his discourses on summer Sabbath afternoons, as well as conducting a modern Hebrew class for adults.

The opening of the community centre has provided a great encouragement to cultural and social activities of all kinds, and an interesting range of adult classes in Jewish subjects and recreational interests is held weekly. Since 1965 Hampstead has taken a leading role in the adult education scheme organised by the Council of Ministers of the United

Synagogue, and in addition a *shiur* is given every Sabbath afternoon, as well as a brief exposition based on the *Shulchan Aruch* at the beginning of the daily morning service. On behalf of the Synagogue, Rabbi S. Sperber conducts a Talmud study circle for an enthusiastic group of local residents.

CHAPTER VIII

Dayan Gollop

As THE YEARS went by, the prospect of A. A. Green's retirement aroused the Synagogue to a sense of anxiety and responsibility in regard to the selection of a successor. Green had been at the helm for so long that it was difficult to imagine Hampstead without him. A special committee was appointed for the purpose of considering the qualifications of suitable ministers from London, the provinces, and abroad. They came to the unanimous conclusion that the name of Dayan Mark Gollop, B.A., should be recommended, and he was duly elected at a meeting in May, 1930.

Dayan Gollop had been minister of the Southend and Westcliff Hebrew Congregation from 1913 to 1923, and had then succeeded Rabbi Sir Hermann Gollancz at the Bayswater Synagogue. At Bayswater he had initiated a number of important congregational activities, and after receiving his rabbinical diploma in 1923 had become a member of the London Beth Din. Since 1926 he had also been the Senior Jewish Chaplain to the Forces. His appointment to Hampstead was important enough on personal grounds, since it brought to the congregation a man of deep piety and human sympathy, but it was all the more significant in that Hampstead, with its tradition of independent thought and its modified service, was now led by an ordained rabbi who was actually a member of the Beth Din.

The enthusiasm and energy with which Dayan Gollop threw himself into the work of the congregation soon showed how he harmonised the rabbinical function with the office of an Anglo-Jewish minister. Talmudic lectures were introduced on summer Sabbath afternoons. A halachic discourse

85

was given in accordance with an old tradition on the Sabbaths before Passover and Yom Kippur, and the eve of Passover was marked by a *siyyum*, or conclusion of a Talmudic tractate.

The founders of the Synagogue, with all their piety, could not have envisaged the Hampstead pulpit as the vehicle for the delivery of rabbinical dialectics.

Dayan Gollop's practical approach to the task of the minister in the community is well summed up in a paper which he gave to the Union of Anglo-Jewish Preachers. He stated :

'I should like to see the community mapped out in definite geographical areas and the Minister of every Synagogue should consider himself the Minister of that area and offer ministration to all and sundry, irrespective of their being seat-holders or not. The Synagogue should come to the homes of people with an offer of religion and not with a demand for money. The psychological effect on the laity would revolutionise their attitude towards religion and the Synagogue. I can conceive of no greater service to Judaism than the implanting into the hearts of men and women that the Synagogue concerns itself with their religious welfare without any expectation of immediate payment. In the long run financial support would be forthcoming in a far greater measure than it is at present, and religion, by ceasing to be a saleable commodity, would be in greater demand than ever.'[1]

The Hampstead community recognised and appreciated their minister's high ideals, and deeply regretted the double blow of war and of ill-health which so soon cut short his efforts to put these ideals into practice.

Dayan Gollop's first year in office brought with it a series of changes in almost all the official personnel of the Synagogue. In 1931 the Rev. W. Stoloff retired and the Rev. Gershon Boyars was appointed to succeed him. Something of Boyars' work is described in the chapter on the Hampstead musical tradition.

Charles Abrahams, who had been beadle since the foundation of the Synagogue, retired in 1930, and in his place Julius Bernstein, then at the New West End Synagogue, became beadle. Mr. Bernstein was born in 1889 and educated in Bradford, where he was honorary secretary of the Hebrew Congregation, and at King's College, London. He served in France and Palestine in the first World War and has long been a leading member of the British Legion. Amongst his wide interests mention must be made of his work for the religious and social welfare of the residents of Levine House, a home for the aged. During the war Mr. Bernstein served as an A.R.P. warden and was known to rush out of the Synagogue at the sound of the sirens, wearing his gold-braided top-hat in place of the routine steel helmet.

In 1930 B. M. Woolf, who had been secretary of the Synagogue for twenty years, was appointed to a similar position at the West London Synagogue, and was succeeded at Hampstead by Nathan Lionel Herman. Born in 1897, Mr. Herman came from a colourful family background. His grandfather was a scholar and kabbalist who featured in Zangwill's 'Children of the Ghetto'. His father was modern languages master at the Central Foundation School and headmaster of the Hampstead Synagogue classes from 1893. After war service Mr. Herman became a senior member of the United Synagogue head office staff before coming to Hampstead. He and his family share a devotion to art and literature, and he is still secretary of the Hampstead Orphan Aid Society, now re-named the Central Orphan Aid Society.

To assist Dayan Gollop, a series of student ministers served Hampstead in these years – the Rev. Philip Cohen, the Rev. Isaac Levy, the Rev. Samuel Venitt, and the Rev. S. Clayman.

As well as changes in personnel, the Synagogue now also saw a revitalisation of communal activities. In particular, the social aspects of congregational life were cultivated. The Hampstead Young People's Association was formed.

A series of Sunday morning talks on religious problems was arranged. The Literary Society which had been founded in 1902 took on new life. A special Children's Synagogue was constructed, thanks to the generosity of several members of the congregation, and was opened by John Lewis at a consecration service in July, 1935, in which a junior members' choir took part. The junior members of the congregation, for whom special Holyday services had been held for some years, were provided with a prayer book compiled and edited by Dayan Gollop, and an order of service was drawn up for use at the annual children's Simchath Torah service.

To provide better accommodation for congregational activities, a hall dedicated to the memory of Samuel Moses was erected and was declared open in May, 1935 by Dr. Jacob Snowman, then the senior past warden. Dr. Snowman said that Samuel Moses had been an honorary officer who showed not an overpowering passion to lead but a sincere and ardent desire to serve. He had possessed classical learning and sound Jewish education. His idea of a Synagogue embraced education, philanthropy and literary activity, and this new hall would provide the means to carry out these purposes. The Samuel Moses Hall was used for overflow services and communal activities for nearly thirty years, but it in its turn became increasingly inadequate and it was replaced by the modern community centre completed in 1964.

After 1933 the course of congregational history was considerably influenced by events in the Jewish communities of Central Europe. In common with other congregations, Hampstead devoted a great deal of energy to the welfare of Jewish immigrants who came to Britain as refugees from Nazi tyranny. An increasing number of German and Austrian Jews were welcomed at services, and eventually a large concentration of Central European Jews settled in the district.[2]

The United Synagogue made facilities available for special

The Rev. Gershon Boyars

The Rev. Dr. Isaac Levy, O.B.E., T.D., B.A.

The Rev. Raymond Apple, B.A., LL.B.

The Rev. Charles Lowy

The Children's Synagogue

services for refugees, which took place chiefly at the Hampstead and Brondesbury Synagogues. The sermons, at first given in German and eventually in English, were preached mainly by Rabbi Dr. Ignaz Maybaum. Some of his sermons were published in a book entitled 'Man and Catastrophe', to which the Archbishop of York contributed a foreword.

After September, 1939, Synagogue activities had to be almost completely suspended because of war conditions. Dayan Gollop, as Senior Jewish Chaplain to the Forces, was immediately called up for service, and the Rev. S. Clayman was appointed temporary Minister of Hampstead, to be followed twelve months later by the Rev. (now Rabbi) Morris Nemeth, who gave five years of devoted service to the Synagogue. A large number of members of the congregation joined the armed forces, some losing their lives in the service of their country. Many other members, and particularly the children, were evacuated from London.

In the summer and autumn of 1940, while London was under continual bombardment from the air, the honorary officers, Leopold Lazarus, Bernard Raperport and I. W. Goldberg, organised a 'Recall to the Synagogue' campaign, and some of the leading members of the ministry, headed by the Chief Rabbi, lectured weekly on this theme to crowded congregations.

Services continued, and though social and cultural activities could not be maintained, much charitable and welfare work was carried out by the ladies of the congregation for people rendered homeless by air raids. Contact was maintained with members through a bulletin issued every few months, as well as by means of parcels of cigarettes and other comforts sent to those serving in the forces. Again, in 1941, a series of addresses in the 'Recall to the Synagogue' campaign was arranged, and in the following two years a series of addresses by prominent laymen, given at the end of the Sabbath morning service, attracted large audiences.

1942 saw the fiftieth anniversary of the establishment of

the Synagogue. A souvenir booklet containing a short history of the congregation by Dr. Jacob Snowman was issued, and a special service was held on Sunday, 6th September, in the presence of the Mayor and Mayoress of Hampstead and other civic and communal dignitaries. The service was conducted by Dayan Gollop, the Revs. G. Boyars, W. Stoloff and M. Nemeth, and the choir under Samuel Alman. The address was given by the Chief Rabbi, who compared Jewish life in 1892 and in 1942, stating that while the founders of the Hampstead Synagogue had not had to face such trials as were besetting Jewry in Nazi-dominated lands, they were men of loyal faith who could face and conquer the spiritual perils of prosperity.

On the general British scene, an outcome of the early period of the war was the formation of the Council of Christians and Jews in 1942 with the aim of combating all forms of racial and religious intolerance. Even before this, however, meetings of Christians and Jews had been held in the Samuel Moses Hall at Hampstead, at the invitation and with the support of Dayan Gollop. After the war, a branch of the Council of Christians and Jews was set up in Hampstead due to the efforts of the Rt. Hon. Anthony Greenwood, the Rev. Dr. Isaac Levy and others. For more than ten years the chairman of this branch has been Mr. Robert Brodtman, a member of the Hampstead Synagogue.

The Minister of the Synagogue has always been regarded as the local spokesman on matters affecting Jewry, and parties of Christian visitors have often been welcomed to the Synagogue services. There can hardly be another Synagogue in the country that has extended hospitality to more non-Jewish visitors than Hampstead. The interior of the Synagogue has also been seen on television by millions of viewers, when the Rev. Dr. Levy presented what was probably the first programme on Jewish religious practices and worship to be arranged by an Anglo-Jewish Minister.

The happiest of relations have always prevailed between

the Jewish and general communities in Hampstead. A
number of members of the congregation have served on the
Hampstead Borough Council, notably Mr. Emanuel Snow-
man, a former mayor, who was made a Freeman of
Hampstead the day before Hampstead, Holborn and St.
Pancras combined in 1965 to form the London Borough
of Camden. In fact, the first Mayor of Camden was Sir
Samuel Fisher, a member of the Jewish community.

By 1943 a number of members had returned to London
and it became possible for the Hebrew classes and children's
Sabbath services to start to function again, and the young
people started a social club. The Synagogue escaped serious
damage from enemy action, though in February 1944, an
air raid put the building out of action for a few months.
The raid took place on a Friday night, but thanks to the
initiative of Julius Bernstein, the beadle, the Samuel Moses
Hall was made ready for service the following morning,
Shabbath Shekalim, on which the Haphtarah referred to the
need to repair the breaches in the wall of the Temple.

In March, 1944, members learned with profound sorrow
that Dayan Gollop had decided, due to ill-health, to retire
prematurely from his position as Minister. Dayan Gollop
hoped that after a prolonged period of rest and recuperation
he would again be able to take part in the spiritual affairs
of the community. This unfortunately did not prove possible,
and after a long illness the Dayan died on 4th August, 1950.
He had integrated himself so closely into the life of Hampstead that members felt, when his retirement was announced,
like a ship without a rudder.

The honorary officers, who were now Bernard Raperport,
Emanuel Snowman and J. C. Gilbert, determined to maintain the Synagogue's vitality, and in order to arouse the interest of the congregation, Dr. Cecil Roth was invited to
address the annual general meeting that year on 'The Re-
Building of Jewish Life'. Dr. Roth declared that he spoke
with a historian's objectivity when he said that no onslaught

upon Jewish existence had ever been as brutal, systematic and destructive as that which was being experienced at that time. They in England were almost the only survivors of European Jewry, and the responsibility which had devolved upon them was tremendous. He was concerned at the decreasing hold and strength of Judaism, and the falling standard of Jewish public life, and the transvaluation of Jewish ethical values. One of the most important proposals he made for rebuilding Jewish life was the re-conversion of the Synagogue into an educational instrument.

By Rosh Hashanah of 1945 the congregation was able to judge whether there was any possibility of implementing these ideas at Hampstead. The cloud had lifted. The ladies' guild and youth club had functioned regularly during the war. The classes, which had again had to close down with the re-evacuation in 1944, could now re-open. The choir was re-organised. The Literary Society was re-constituted. And the Synagogue was able to welcome back from war service many young people whose interest in the congregation – as shown, for instance, by the fact that seven of them were elected to the board of management at the next annual meeting – was an encouraging sign and a denial of the communal rumours that the young people had come back uninterested in religion and disillusioned with it.

CHAPTER IX

The Last Twenty Years

IN JANUARY, 1946 applications were invited for the vacant post of minister. The selection committee looked for a man who would fit in with the congregation, who would appeal to all classes of members, in particular the young men and women returning from the Forces, and who could organise the children and youth.

Their decision was to recommend the Rev. Isaac Levy, who had been a student minister at Hampstead under Dayan Gollop from 1934–36 and had subsequently been minister at Hampstead Garden Suburb (1936–38) and Bayswater (from 1938). He had been the first minister to volunteer for military service in 1939, and his first assignment was to the refugee camp of the Pioneer Corps in Richborough, Kent. He had later served as Senior Chaplain in the Middle East and in Germany and played a large part in the organisation of relief services in the Belsen concentration camp. One of his fellow chaplains said of his war service that 'in his sincerity he was like a Hillel, in courage like an Akiba, and in friendship like a Jonathan'.

He was inducted into office at Hampstead by Rabbi Israel Brodie, then the Senior Jewish Chaplain, on 29th June, 1946. In his induction address the new minister said that the great task confronting Jewry was that of physical and spiritual reconstruction after the tragic events of the previous thirteen years. His aim would be to foster an all-embracing congregational activity which would restore the Synagogue to its rightful place as the centre of Jewish life and would inspire Anglo-Jewry to become creative.

Two major tasks had to be faced at Hampstead. The

93

Synagogue building still bore the scars of the damage it had sustained during the war, and efforts now had to be made to reinstate the Synagogue and restore it to its former beauty. The minister was responsible for the creation of a small committee called the Art Committee which launched a competition for designs for the stained-glass windows. The members of this committee were Alderman Emanuel Snowman, his son Kenneth, and the Rev. Isaac Levy. Ultimately the designs submitted by Mr. B. Sochachewsky were accepted and the windows which now adorn the Synagogue replaced those originally designed by Solomon J. Solomon.

Perhaps a bigger challenge was that of reconstructing communal life. Activities for various age groups were energetically arranged, the Literary Society was reinvigorated, an imaginative series of Sabbath afternoon lectures was instituted, and a Synagogue magazine (at first called the Hampstead Synagogue Review but now named 'Rivon') made its appearance.

In 1948 Dr. Levy succeeded Rabbi Brodie as Senior Jewish Chaplain to H.M. Forces, and held that office for a longer period than any of his predecessors, retiring in 1966. In view of the responsibilities of the chaplaincy, Dr. Levy was now relieved of some of his routine congregational duties by a succession of assistant ministers, in each case senior students of Jews' College. They included the Rev. (now Rabbi) Joseph Shaw, the Rev. (now Rabbi) Ronald Lubofsky, the Rev. Norman Gale and the Rev. Edward L. Jackson.

It is worthy of note that Dayan Harris M. Lazarus was a regular worshipper at Hampstead for a number of years until his death in 1962. He assisted in the services from time to time, particularly with blowing the *shofar,* and endeared himself to the congregation as a wise and tolerant soul. Another senior member of the ministry, the Rev. Jacob Israelstam, formerly of Bradford, has been associated with Hampstead since his retirement in 1961.

The Hampstead pulpit under Dr. Levy – a powerful personality and a forceful preacher – became a vehicle for free and open expression on all matters affecting current events in the Jewish and general communities, even though at times this raised some measure of controversy. The pulpit was frequently occupied by eminent visitors, and particular mention must be made of a notable series of pulpit addresses on 'The Challenge of Historical Judaism to our Time' given in 1951 by Chief Rabbi Israel Brodie, the Rev. Ephraim Levine, the Rev. Dr. Abraham Cohen, the Rev. Emmanuel Drukker and Dr. Levy, and later published in booklet form.

Dr. Levy was awarded the O.B.E. in 1953 and the T.D. in 1964. In 1956 he became a Doctor of Philosophy of the University of London for a thesis on 'Rabbi Ishmael ben Elisha (59–133 C.E.): his Life and Teaching'. His other writings include 'A Guide to Passover' (1958) and 'The Synagogue: its History and Function' (1964). Since 1946, when he assumed the chairmanship of the Education Department of the Jewish National Fund, he has been responsible for the production of educational material for children and aids for teachers, which are widely used throughout the English-speaking world.

During his term of office as President of the Union of Anglo-Jewish Preachers Dr. Levy established the Association of Ministers (Preachers) of the United Synagogue and was its chairman for six years. This Association became the first medium for direct negotiations between the ministry and the honorary officers of the United Synagogue, and upon its chairman devolved the responsibility of raising the status of the ministry and of fighting the battles of the clergy.

For several years Dr. Levy was honorary secretary of Jews' College and lecturer in homiletics, but in 1962 he resigned from both offices in protest against the decision of the Chief Rabbi not to appoint Rabbi Dr. Louis Jacobs as principal of the College. Two years later, further controversy surrounded Dr. Jacobs, who, because of views challenging the

95

divinity and Mosaic authorship of the Pentateuch was not permitted to return to his former position as minister of the New West End Synagogue, and Dr. Levy again strongly supported him in a number of outspoken statements.

Eventually a new congregation, the New London Synagogue, was established by Dr. Jacobs' supporters in the building in Abbey Road, N.W.8, which had housed the St. John's Wood Synagogue until 1964.

In 1955, Julius Bernstein, the beadle at Hampstead, retired from office after twenty-five years' service. His successors have been Horace Haft, Harry Scott, David Hinden and, today, Stanley Kershaw. In the interval between the appointment of each one Mr. Bernstein has come out of retirement and returned to duty. The present beadle, Mr. Kershaw, was born and educated in Germany, served in the British army, later lived in Bolivia, where he was active in Jewish and municipal affairs, and is now in business in London in addition to his part-time position at the Synagogue.

In 1959, the Rev. Gershon Boyars retired after twenty-eight years as chazan and was succeeded by the Rev. Charles Lowy, then with the Queen's Park Synagogue in Glasgow. A further change in Synagogue personnel came in 1962, when Nathan Lionel Herman, the secretary, retired. Phineas L. May, secretary of the Bayswater Synagogue, was appointed in his place. Mr. May has had a long family association with Hampstead, and before the second World War was on the staff of the United Synagogue in charge of what was then known as the organisation department. For many years he has been actively interested in Jewish youth work, and is also a talented artist and cartoonist. He administers the widespread activities of the Synagogue with energy, efficiency and humour.

At the end of 1964 Dr. Levy submitted his resignation from his position as minister. He had been invited to become director of the Jewish National Fund in Britain, and stated in a letter to Maurice Sanders, the warden president, that he felt this would give him an opportunity to devote himself to the cause of Israel, which had always been dear to his heart.

The Rev. Raymond Apple was appointed minister in his place – following in something of a tradition, for like Dayan Gollop and Dr. Levy, as well as Mr. Phineas May and the late Mr. Harry Scott, he came to Hampstead from the historic Bayswater Synagogue. Hampstead over the years has had many links with Bayswater, not only these personal ones, but links in outlook too, for both have stood for a middle-of-the-road philosophy, a dignified mode of worship, and a tradition of service to the community.

Mr. Apple was born in Australia and graduated in arts and law at Melbourne University before coming to London to study at Jews' College. In Australia he was headmaster of the United Jewish Education Board, Melbourne, and the initiator and organiser of a widespread system of correspondence lessons for Jewish children living in 'outback' areas of Australia and New Zealand – some of them fifty miles from their nearest neighbour and 500 miles from the nearest Synagogue. In London, he was for four years Religious Director of the Association for Jewish Youth before going to Bayswater. Like his predecessors at Hampstead he is active in a variety of causes in the Jewish and general communities. He was inducted into office at Hampstead on 9th May, 1965, by Chief Rabbi Israel Brodie.

The highlight of recent years in congregational history has been the erection of the modern community centre adjoining the Synagogue. After the war it was suggested that part of the house in Fawley Road, N.W.6, where Dayan Gollop had lived, should become a social centre for the congregation. But the idea proved impracticable and the congregational societies, as well as the Hebrew classes, had to make do with the Samuel Moses Hall and the other rooms which had been added at various earlier periods when the Synagogue building was extended.

It was not only due to increased membership that this accommodation became more and more inadequate, but it was also a reflection of wider concept of the Synagogue as a *beth am* – a house of the people – providing not simply a place of worship but also a centre for social and cultural meeting. It became obvious by the end of the 1950's that Hampstead would benefit from a specially built *beth am* with adequate facilities for a wide variety of activities.

The idea was launched by Dr. Levy at a Simchath Torah reception, and he immediately proceeded to set the wheels in motion to translate it into practical terms. A site in Dennington Park Road next to the Synagogue was acquired and a large-scale fund-raising campaign launched. In November, 1962, the foundation stone of the community centre building was laid by I. W. Goldberg who, with Dr. Levy, was responsible for raising most of the money required, and the centre was completed and consecrated in November, 1964. It has four floors, with a large main hall, a smaller hall, a library, various meeting rooms and well-equipped classrooms, as well as a modern kitchen. Today it houses activities catering for every age group and interest in their range is indicated by the following list :

Adult education courses

Art class (in conjunction with the Marylebone Institute)

Blind Society

B'nai Akiva (for children)

Bridge Club

Brownies (for girls)

Chess Club

Choir Committee

C o o k e r y demonstration courses (in conjunction with the Marylebone Institute)

Friendly Circle (for 30-60 age group)

Friendship Club (for over-60 age group)

Hampstead Jewish Centre Club (for over-30 age group)

Hampstead Film Workshop (creative film - making group)

Hampstead Y.U.S.A. (for 18-25 age group)

Hebrew and Religion Classes (for children)

Hebrew conversation circle

Ladies' Guild

Magazine Committee

Parents' Association

Sewing circle

Study group (for young people)

Talmud Shiur

Youth Club (for 14-16 age group)

Notes

The following archive material in the possession of the Synagogue has been drawn upon for the purpose of this history:

Pre-1892

Minutes of (*a*) the General Committee, 1889–1891
         (*b*) the Executive Committee, 1889–1890
         (*c*) the Building Committee, 1891
         (*d*) the Officials Sub-Committee, 1892
         (*e*) the Committee concerned with the Foundation Stone ceremony, 1892

Report on the Form of Service, 1889

The Book of the Fair, 1891

Order of Service at the Laying of the Foundation Stone, 1892

Order of Service at the Consecration of the Synagogue, 1892

Correspondence, papers and documents of the years 1889–1892, mostly concerned with Herbert Bentwich and his association with the Synagogue

Post-1892

Minutes of (*a*) General Meetings, 1892 to date
         (*b*) the Board of Management, 1892 to date
         (*c*) the Ritual Sub-Committee, 1892
         (*d*) the Choir Committee, 1895 to date
         (*e*) the Classes Committee, 1891 to date

Miscellaneous Minute Book, 1911–1914

Draft Minute Book, 1914–1925

Printed Annual Reports for certain years

Souvenir Order of Service and History, 25th Anniversary, 1917

Souvenir Order of Service and History, 50th Anniversary, 1942

Printed circulars and bulletins, 1930–1946
The Hampstead Synagogue Review, 1954–1959
Rivon, 1960 to date
Printed Membership Lists of the congregation
Use has also been made of the issues of the *Jewish Chronicle* covering the whole period, but particularly for the years 1889–1892.

INTRODUCTION

1. *Jewish Chronicle*, 4th March, 1892, p. 9.

2. *ibid.*, 11th March, 1892, p. 7. A similar view was expressed by Bentwich's colleague, Frank I. Lyons, in his address at the laying of the foundation stone of the Synagogue on 13th March, 1892, when he said that at the time of the controversy in 1889 he had felt, and now still held, 'that all reasonable concessions might be obtained within the United Synagogue.'

3. *The New London Spy: A Discreet Guide to the City's Pleasures*, ed. by Hunter Davies, London, 1966, p. 268.

CHAPTER I

1. The district was inhabited at least as early as Roman times. A Roman road leading to St. Albans crossed the Heath, and Roman pottery was discovered near Hampstead Wells in the eighteenth century. The document supposedly issued by Edgar the Peaceable contains the first written reference to Hampstead, though the fact that Edgar died in 975 casts doubt on the authenticity of the document. A comprehensive collection of material about Hampstead is to be found in the local history section of the Central Library, Swiss Cottage. The standard work is Thomas J. Barratt's *The Annals of Hampstead*, 3 vols., London, 1912.

2. William Howitt, *The Northern Heights of London: or Historical Associations of Hampstead, Highgate, Muswell Hill, Hornsey, and Islington*, London, 1869, p. 122.

3. (Daniel Defoe), *A Tour Through the Whole Island of Great Britain, By A Gentleman*, first published 1724–1726; revised ed. in Everyman's Library, London, 2 vols., 1962: vol. 2, p. 3.

Nine editions were published between 1724 and 1778, but after Defoe's death in 1731 successive editors made some changes in the text. In some editions the reference to Jews was omitted. On the Mendes da Costa family, see Albert M. Hyamson, *The Sephardim of England*, London, 1951, chapter VII: 'Some Eighteenth-Century Personalities.'

4. Like Defoe, John Macky, in his *Journey Through England*, 1714, claims that 'Hampstead . . . seems to be overstock'd with Jews' (cited by Cecil Roth, *Essays and Portraits in Anglo-Jewish History*, Philadelphia, 1962, p. 242). Defoe and Macky both exaggerated the extent of Jewish influence in Hampstead (see the next note). It is well known that Defoe had little sympathy for Jews: see Harold Fisch, *The Dual Image: A Study of the Figure of the Jew in English Literature*, London, 1959, p. 42; M. F. Modder, *The Jew in the Literature of England*, Philadelphia, 1960, pp. 50–51, 372; Edgar Rosenberg, *From Shylock to Svengali: Jewish Stereotypes in English Fiction*, London, 1961, pp. 44, 76, 322.

5. *Index* to minute books of the Court of the Manor of Hampstead dealing with land transactions, vol. A: 1742–1782; vol. B: 1783–1809; *Hampstead Return of Population*, 1801 and 1811; Lists of principal residents given in an Act of 1774 for the lighting of Hampstead, an Act of 1800 concerning poor law administration in Hampstead, and an Act of 1821 concerning the repair of roads leading to Hampstead and Highgate. Of course it is possible that the Jews to whom Defoe and Macky referred were living outside the official boundaries of Hampstead and closer to Highgate.

6. Cecil Roth, 'The First Jew in Hampstead', *Jewish Chronicle*, 28th October, 1932; reprinted as *Jewish Museum Publications*, no. 1, 1932, and in *Essays and Portraits*, loc. cit., p. 242.

7. The beginnings of the St. John's Wood Synagogue may be traced back to a letter, signed 'An Earnest Jew', in the *Jewish Chronicle*, 3rd April, 1868, p. 5, which claims that there 'is a very large Jewish population in the neighbourhood of Regent's Park, Hampstead, St. John's Wood, Portland Town, Camden Town West, Haverstock Hill, and a large district densely covered with houses, and inhabited by a very large proportion of our community.' The writer calls for the formation of a committee to work for the erection of a Synagogue in the district, and some support was shown in letters published in the following week's *Chronicle*. The matter was raised at precisely the time that the three City Synagogues were considering proposals for the establishment of the United Synagogue, and it was hoped that the new body would be able to sponsor the erection of Synagogues in districts where they were needed. By 1872, however, the proposals for a Synagogue in St. John's Wood had to be temporarily abandoned due to lack of support (*Jewish Chronicle*, 26th April, 1872, p. 5). Eventually a temporary building was erected in 1876, to be succeeded by a permanent structure in 1882 (see H. L. Price, 'History of the Synagogue', in *Order of Service at the Re-Consecration of the St. John's Wood Synagogue*, 13th March, 1921).

8. Norman and Margery Bentwich, *Herbert Bentwich, the Pilgrim Father*, Jerusalem (n.d.), p. 67; cf. Norman Bentwich, 'The Wanderers and Other Jewish Scholars of My Youth', presidential address to Jewish Historical Society of England, 9th November, 1960 (*J.H.S.E. Transactions*, vol. 20, p. 51).

9. In ancient times an annual cycle, whereby the whole of the Pentateuch was covered in one year, was in vogue in Babylon, and a triennial cycle in Palestine. The triennial cycle was superseded in the Middle Ages. An interesting Anglo-Jewish document on the subject is the *Report on the Sabbath Reading of the Scriptures in a Triennial Cycle*, issued by a special committee of inquiry of the New West End Synagogue in 1913.

10. *Jewish Chronicle*, 11th March, 1892, p. 7.

11. *ibid.*, 19th July, 1889, p. 9; 26th July, 1889, p. 4; 8th November, 1889, p. 5.

12. See Morris Joseph, *Order of Prayer as used at the Sabbath Afternoon Service at Hampstead*, with an English paraphrase of the Hebrew text, London, 1890. Morris Joseph, who was living at the time in St. John's Wood, had been minister of the North London Synagogue from 1868–1874 and of the Old Hebrew Congregation, Liverpool, from 1874–1882. He resigned from the Liverpool position to take a long rest after a breakdown in health.

13. In an address on 'Higher Judaism' given by Oswald John Simon at the Sabbath afternoon service on 19th March, 1892, he stated: 'The movement of which these services are the embodiment, fills a vacant gap, and is the first sign of religious revival for over fifty years. It was never conceived in the spirit of party or of division . . . This model Jewish service might be held in different districts of London, and thus present a lesson of what is meant by a solemn and reverent worship.'

14. The Annual Report of the St. John's Wood Synagogue for 1892 states that the organisers of the Sabbath afternoon services had asked for the use of that Synagogue and were prepared to forego the use of the organ if this permission were granted. The Chief Rabbi, however, laid down other conditions, which the organisers of the services would not agree to meet.

15. Morris Joseph, *The Ideal in Judaism and Other Sermons Preached during* 1890–91–92, London, 1893. Some of the sermons delivered by others at the Sabbath afternoon services are given in Israel Abrahams and Claude G. Montefiore, *Aspects of Judaism: being Eighteen Sermons*, London, 1895.

CHAPTER II

1. Though the Chief Rabbi objected to a mixed choir singing at the laying of the foundation stone, the Hampstead committee understood from him that once the Synagogue had been established it might be possible to arrange for a mixed choir of members, which could then come under the category of congregational singing. The inconsistency was duly noticed by Israel Zangwill, who wrote in *Children of the Ghetto* (Book II, Chapter 9), published at this period, that the Rabbinate, experiencing 'grave difficulties in reconciling all parties to its rule', pronounced that 'an organisation of mixed voices was allowable, but not a mixed choir.' In its editorial of 26th August, 1892, the *Jewish Chronicle* remarks caustically: 'Women's voices are . . . tabooed, though they may lose their objectionable character when the Chief Rabbi is not within ear-shot.'

2. *Jewish Chronicle*, 18th March, 1892, pp. 9–11. An article about Delissa Joseph, the architect, appeared in *The Builders' Journal* of 3rd March, 1896, together with a picture of the Hampstead Synagogue. The article stated, 'Mr. Joseph has for some years made a special study of Synagogue plan and design, his most successful work in this direction being the Hampstead Synagogue, believed to be the first Synagogue in the Kingdom planned on the basis of an octagon, and the first in which the Continental method was adopted of placing the reading platform, pulpit and ark at one end of the building.' Cf. Edward Jamilly, 'Anglo-Jewish Architects and Architecture in the 18th and 19th Centuries', *J.H.S.E. Transactions*, vol. 18, p. 127.

3. Morris Joseph, *Judaism as Creed and Life*, London, 1903; 4th ed., 1958, p. vii.

4. See *Jewish Chronicle*, June and July, 1892. It is interesting to note that when Joseph was invited by the St. John's Wood Synagogue, of which he was a member, to preach there in October, 1892, the Chief Rabbi would not give his assent, stating that 'circumstances have changed since the time when he last preached in your Synagogue'.

5. At the West London Synagogue prayers for the restoration of sacrifices had been said from the establishment of the Synagogue in 1842 until about forty years later (D. W. Marks, *Jubilee Address* on 27th January, 1892) but had now been discontinued.

6. In this connection, Chief Rabbi J. H. Hertz (*Commentary to the Authorised Daily Prayer Book*, one-vol. ed., London, 1947, pp. 532–533) endorses the views on the *Amidah* of Dr. Michael Friedländer of Jews' College: 'Let him whose heart is not with his fellow-worshippers in any of their supplications, silently substitute his own prayers for them; but let him not interfere with the devotion of those to whom "the statutes of the Lord are right, rejoicing the heart; the commandments of the Lord pure, enlightening the eyes; the judgments of the Lord true and righteous altogether" (Ps. ٤9:9–10), and who yearn for the opportunity of fulfilling Divine commandments which they cannot observe at present.'

7. In spite of the controversies over the liturgy at this period, a unifying force has always been the *Authorised Daily Prayer Book* edited and translated by Simeon Singer and first issued in 1890. In 1962 a revised edition was published, and the Chief Rabbi's revision committee included only two lay members, both of them members of the Hampstead Synagogue—Mr. Hugh Harris and Dr. Leonard V. Snowman.

8. Michael Adler, *The History of the Hammersmith Synagogue*, London, 1950: part I: 1890–1903.

9. Olga Somech Phillips, *Solomon J. Solomon: A Memoir of Peace and War*, London (n.d.), pp. 87–88 re the Solomon family and Hampstead.

10. From time to time during the present century suggestions have been made for the further beautification of the building. One plan, deferred because of the first World War, was realised in 1924 when a new marble and alabaster Ark and *bimah* were constructed and the pillars of the Synagogue enclosed in marble. The old wooden Ark and *bimah* were presented to the Ealing and Acton District Synagogue. Several sets of stained-glass windows were also installed at different periods, mostly in memory of past members of the congregation. The first window of the series on the ground floor depicting the twelve tribes of Israel was presented by the Rev. and Mrs. A. A. Green in memory of their son, Alan Laurence Green.

11. *Herbert Bentwich: the Pilgrim Father*, loc. cit., pp. 65–66.

CHAPTER III

1. A penetrating analysis of the situation appears in Israel Zangwill's *Children of the Ghetto* (loc. cit.) in a chapter describing the impact of '*The Flag of Judah*, price one penny, largest circulation of any Jewish organ.' Zangwill writes: 'Among the discussions which rent the body politic . . . were also the grave questions of English and harmoniums in the Synagogue, of the confirmation of girls and their utilisation in the choir. The Rabbinate, whose grave difficulties in reconciling all parties to its rule were augmented by the existence of the *Flag*, pronounced it heinous to introduce English excerpts into the liturgy; if, however, they were not read from the central platform, they were legitimate; harmoniums were permissible, but only during special services, and an organisation of mixed voices was allowable, but not a mixed choir; children might be confirmed, but the word "confirmation" should be avoided. Poor Rabbinate! The politics of the little community were extremely complex. What with rabid zealots yearning for the piety of the good old times, spiritually-minded ministers working with uncomfortable earnestness for a larger Judaism, radicals dropping out, moderates clamouring for quiet, and schismatics organising new and tiresome movements, the Rabbinate could scarcely do aught else than emit sonorous platitudes and remain in office.' There is more than a hint of Hampstead here, as well as a clear indication that before long a more radical movement would make its appearance.

2. Accounts of the early years of the J.R.U. are given in Claude G. Montefiore, 'The Liberal Movement in English Jewry', in *Central Conference of American Rabbis Yearbook*, vol. 20 (1910), pp. 176–196; *The Liberal Jewish Monthly*, issues in

memory of Montefiore, September, 1938 and June, 1958; Lily H. Montagu, 'The History of Liberal Judaism in England', in *Judaean Addresses*, vol. IV, N.Y., 1933, pp. 152–162; *Jewish Addresses delivered at the services of the Jewish Religious Union during the first session*, 1902–3, London, 1904. Hermann Adler explained his attitude to the movement in his famous sermon, *The Old Paths*, delivered at the St. John's Wood Synagogue on 6th December, 1902. I am grateful to Mr. J. M. Duparc, formerly secretary of the Liberal Jewish Synagogue, for information on A. A. Green's association with the movement.

CHAPTER IV

1. See Ruth P. Lehmann, *Jews' College Library: A History*, London, 2nd ed., 1967.

2. A revealing commentary on the outlook of Green's generation on matters which today are treated without embarrassment is provided by his translation of the popular madrigal, *Echad Mi Yodea*, 'Who Knows One?' In the Hebrew text the number nine is represented by *tisha yarchei ledah*, 'nine are the months of child-bearing'. Green substituted the phrase, 'nine Jewish feasts' and proceeded to list nine feasts in a footnote (p. 101), claiming that this was 'more in consonance with our modern ideas of what is adapted for the perusal of children' (p. 4).

3. In his sermon on 19th November, 1892, Green said of his work in the East End: 'This work lies very near to my heart. I know the East of London. I was born there, was there brought up, and there was always taught to look with pity upon the burdens of my brethren. What I have seen and what I have known have left an impression upon my mind so deep that ever since I have realised what are the magnificent opportunities of a Jewish minister I have looked forward to work in the metropolis as affording occasion to help a little in the great labour of love that grows for us day by day.'

4. *Report of the Second Conference of Anglo-Jewish Preachers*, London, 1925, pp. 40, 51.

5. *The Jewish Chronicle, 1841–1941: A Century of Newspaper History*, London, 1949, pp. 136–8.

6. 'Some of Our Difficulties', in *Three Addresses on Jewish Religious Education*, London, 1929.

CHAPTER V

1. Stoloff's publications were: *Shir Ush'vocho (Song and Praise): A Handbook of Music arranged for Synagogue, Religion Class and Home*, London, 1912; *Songs and Prayers of Israel* (written by Stoloff and the Rev. A. Perlzweig), London, 1914; *Inauguration of the Sabbath, and Friday Evening Service, in Hebrew and English, set to Music*, London, 1930.

CHAPTER VII

1. Opening Address to Second Conference of Anglo-Jewish Preachers, 1925.

2. A children's Simchath Torah service was held for a number of years on the afternoon of Shemini Atzereth. This practice was re-introduced in 1966 and Dayan Gollop's Order of Service was revised for the occasion.

CHAPTER VIII

1. I. Livingstone, *The Union of Anglo-Jewish Preachers: A Retrospect*, with extracts from talks given by members at some of the meetings, London, 1949, p. 13.

2. Some eventually joined the Hampstead Synagogue; many became associated with the New Liberal Congregation in Belsize Square, N.W.3, established in 1939.

Glossary

AMIDAH (Lit., 'standing'): a series of benedictions found in a central position in every Jewish service. On all occasions except the evening service it is recited silently by the worshipper and then repeated by the Reader.

ALMEMAR (or BIMAH): platform from which the service is conducted.

ARBA'AH MINIM (Lit., 'four species'): plants used during services on Sukkoth to symbolise the bounty of a good harvest.

ASHKENAZI (Lit., 'German'): deriving from Eastern or Central Europe, in contrast to Sephardi (from Spain or Portugal). There are slight differences between the Ashkenazi and Sephardi ritual and pronunciation of Hebrew.

BARECHU (Lit., 'Bless!'): a call to congregational worship in the morning and evening services.

BAR MITZVAH (Lit., 'son of the commandment'): male Jew aged 13 or over on whom the performance of the religious precepts is obligatory.

BIRKATH KOHANIM (Lit., 'blessing of the priests'): ceremony in which the formula of Numbers 6 : 24-26 is invoked.

CHANUKAH : (Lit., 'dedication'): commemoration of the victory of the Maccabees.

CHAZAN : cantor, precentor.

CHUKKATH HAGOYIM : non-Jewish usage.

DUCHAN (Lit., 'platform'): originally, the platform from which the Birkath Kohanim was pronounced; now applied to the ceremony itself.

EIN KAMOCHA (Lit., 'there is none like Thee'): opening phrase of the ceremony in which the Scroll of the Torah is taken from the Ark.

111

HAGGADAH (Lit., 'narration'): home service on first two evenings of Passover.

HALACHAH (Lit., 'way'): Jewish law.

HAPHTARAH (Lit., 'conclusion'): reading from the Prophets.

KIDDUSH (Lit., 'sanctification'): prayer over wine recited at commencement of the meal on Sabbaths and festivals.

KOHANIM (Lit., 'priests'): Jews credited with descent from Aaron.

MINCHAH (Lit., 'meal-offering'): afternoon service.

MINHAG: custom.

MINYAN: quorum of ten adult males required for public prayer.

MI SHEBERACH (Lit., 'He who blessed'): prayer for an individual worshipper.

MUSAPH: additional service on Sabbaths and Festivals.

NER TAMID: perpetual lamp in Synagogue.

NISHMATH (Lit., 'the breath of every being'): beginning of a section of the Sabbath morning service.

PESACH: Passover, commemorating the Exodus from Egypt.

POSEKIM: authorities on Jewish law.

PURIM (Lit., 'lots'): commemoration of events recorded in Book of Esther.

ROSH HASHANAH: New Year.

SHACHARITH: morning service.

SHAVUOTH: Pentecost or Feast of Weeks.

SHIVAH (Lit., 'seven'): week of mourning.

SHOFAR: ram's-horn trumpet used in New Year services.

SHULCHAN ARUCH (Lit., 'prepared table'): code of Jewish law.

SIDRA: lesson from the Pentateuch.

SIMCHATH TORAH (Lit., 'rejoicing of the Torah'): conclusion and recommencement of annual cycle of Torah readings.

SUKKOTH: festival of Tabernacles.

TALMUD (Lit., 'learning'): greatest work of Jewish literature after the Bible.

TORAH: Pentateuch; Jewish teaching in general.

YOM KIPPUR: Day of Atonement.

Officers of the Congregation
1967

Minister
The Rev. RAYMOND APPLE, B.A., LL.B.

Chazan
The Rev. CHARLES LOWY

Secretary
PHINEAS L. MAY

Beadle
STANLEY KERSHAW

Choirmaster
WILLY SCHARF

Headmaster
ADRIAN WEITZMAN

Wardens
OSCAR SWAN
JONAS SHAW

Financial Representative
Dr. HENRY STOLL

Board of Management

NORMAN ALEXANDER	BERNARD GOLDBERG
Dr. ISAAC B. BAJER	ARTHUR HARINGMAN, F.C.A.
SIDNEY BLOCH	PERCY A. MELLER
EDWARD L. COHN, D.F.C.	RONALD C. MOLYNEUX
Dr. STANLEY ELLISON	Dr. LIONEL STOLL
BERNARD FRIEND, F.C.A.	ALAN WEBBER, B.SC.

113

Representatives at United Synagogue Council

CLIVE E. FEATHER
ISRAEL FINESTEIN, M.A.
JOSEPH C. GILBERT
SYDNEY GOLDBERG
CLAUDE GREEN
ELLIS JOSEPHS

JACK J. LYNN
IAN SCOTT
EMANUEL SNOWMAN, M.V.O.,
   O.B.E., J.P.
ALBERT WOLLMAN

114

Past Honorary Officers

1892–1901	FRANK I. LYONS
1892–94	H. BENTWICH, LL.B.
1892–94	JOHN MEREDITH
1894–96	HENRY NATHAN
1894–1905	SAMUEL MOSES, M.A.
1897–1903	ALEXANDER JACOB
1901–07	CARL STETTAUER
1903–08	ABRAHAM DAVIS
1904–09	DR. JACOB SNOWMAN
1907–13	EMIL KAHN
1908–15	S. M. HEILBUT
1909–16	GEORGE G. JACOB
1913–19	ROBERT S. MOSELY
1915–21	ISIDORE J. ROZELAAR
1916–23	D. MAGNUS
1919–25	S. T. COHN
1921–23	LIONEL TUCK
1923–27	LAWRENCE LEVY
1924–29	A. J. JACOBS

1925–31	JOHN LEWIS
1927–33	HENRY GLEDHILL
1929–35	AARON JACKSON
1931–37	HENRY M. COHEN
1933–39	GEORGE J. TIBBER
1935–41	LEOPOLD LAZARUS
1937–47	BERNARD RAPERPORT
1939–43	ISAAC W. GOLDBERG
1942–49	EMANUEL SNOWMAN
1944–51	JOSEPH C. GILBERT
1947–53	MARK KLEINER
1949–55	MICHAEL ABRAHAMS
1951–57	CLAUDE GREEN
1953–59	JOSEPH PHILLIPS
1955–61	ELLIS JOSEPHS
1957–63	HARRY SUMERAY
1959–63	CYRIL M. ABELSON
1961–66	MAURICE SANDERS

Index

117

118

119